Poetry Workshop

Michael & Peter Benton

Hodder & Stoughton

A MEMBER OF THE HODDER HEADLINE GROUP

Order queries: Please contact Bookpoint Ltd, 39 Milton Park, Abingdon, Oxon OX14 4TD. Telephone: (44) 01235 400414. Fax: (44) 01235 400454. Lines are open from 9 am - 6 pm Monday to Saturday, with a 24-hour message answering service. Email address: orders@bookpoint.co.uk

British Library Cataloguing in Publication Data

Benton, Michael
  Poetry Workshop. – 2Rev.ed
  I. Title   II. Benton
  821

ISBN 0 340 62734 4

First published 1995
Impression number   10 9 8 7 6 5 4 3 2
Year   2004 2003 2002 2001 2000 1999 1998

Typeset by Wearset, Boldon, Tyne and Wear
Printed in Great Britain for Hodder & Stoughton Educational, a division of Hodder Headline Plc, 338, Euston Road, London NW1 3BH by Redwood Books, Trowbridge, Wiltshire.

Contents

Index of Authors

Preface

Poetry Workshop is a source book of ideas and materials for work in English with students at key stages 3 and 4. We hope that teachers will find here a flexible and imaginative approach which also makes considerable literary demands on students.

The book is divided into two parts: Part A is a thematically arranged anthology, each section of which includes its own 'Workshop' ideas. Part B introduces readers to the work of eight poets and suggests project activities to help students develop their own knowledge of these writers.

The book is deliberately 'activities based'. Through its six Workshops, it opens up a varied programme of discussion, drama, and creative and critical writing, the aim of which is to suggest starting points for activities which we hope will be enjoyable and also offer something to students over a wide range of abilities. Accordingly, most of the Workshops invite students to talk in small groups. Informal discussion and individual choice are also encouraged.

We hope that teachers using this book will exploit at least some of the opportunities for varied teaching methods which we suggest in the Workshops. Limited space and a desire not to presume to dictate lessons mean that these sections are fairly short and *must* be expanded and modified, according to the individual situation. We are well aware that by encouraging a more flexible approach we are also encouraging more organisational problems for the teacher. At the risk of being too prescriptive, therefore, we frequently give specific details of how classes or groups might be arranged, in the belief that the vast majority of students need a firm framework before they can explore their own freedom of choice most profitably.

MICHAEL AND PETER BENTON

Man and Beast

CARING FOR ANIMALS

I ask sometimes why these small animals
With bitter eyes, why we should care for them.

I question the sky, the serene blue water,
But it cannot say. It gives no answer.

And no answer releases in my head
A procession of grey shades patched and whimpering,

Dogs with clipped ears, wheezing cart horses
A fly without shadow and without thought.

Is it with these menaces to our vision
With this procession led by a man carrying wood

We must be concerned? The holy land, the rearing
Green island should be kindlier than this.

Yet the animals, our ghosts, need tending to.
Take in the whipped cat and the blinded owl;

Take up the man-trapped squirrel upon your shoulder.
Attend to the unnecessary beasts.

From growing mercy and a moderate love
Great love for the human animal occurs.

And your love grows. Your great love grows and grows.

JON SILKIN

There is a wolf in me . . . fangs pointed for tearing gashes . . .
a red tongue for raw meat . . . and the hot lapping of
blood – I keep this wolf because the wilderness gave it to
me and the wilderness will not let it go.

There is a fox in me . . . a silver-gray fox . . . I sniff and
guess . . . I pick things out of the wind and air . . . I nose in
the dark night and take sleepers and eat them and hide the
feathers . . . I circle and loop and double-cross.

There is a hog in me . . . a snout and a belly . . . a machinery
for eating and grunting . . . a machinery for sleeping
satisfied in the sun – I got this too from the wilderness and
the wilderness will not let it go.

There is a fish in me . . . I know I came from the salt-blue
water-gates . . . I scurried with shoals of herring . . . I blew
waterspouts with porpoises . . . before land was . . . before
the water went down . . . before Noah . . . before the first
chapter of Genesis.

There is a baboon in me . . . clambering-clawed . . .
dog-faced . . . yawping a galoot's* hunger . . . hairy under   *rough lout
the armpits . . . here are the hawk-eyed hankering men . . .
here are the blond and blue-eyed women . . . here they
hide curled asleep waiting . . . ready to snarl and kill . . .
ready to sing and give milk . . . waiting – I keep the
baboon because the wilderness says so.

There is an eagle in me and a mockingbird . . . and the eagle
flies among the Rocky Mountains of my dreams and
fights among the Sierra crags of what I want . . . and the
mockingbird warbles in the early forenoon before the dew
is gone, warbles in the underbrush of my Chattanoogas
of hope, gushes over the blue Ozark foothills of my
wishes – And I got the eagle and the mockingbird from the
wilderness.

O, I got a zoo, I got a menagerie, inside my ribs, under my
bony head, under my red-valve heart – and I got something
else: it is a man-child heart, a woman-child heart: it is a
father and mother and lover: it came from God-Knows-
Where: it is going to God-Knows-Where – For I am the
keeper of the zoo: I say yes and no: I sing and kill and
work: I am a pal of the world. I came from the wilderness.

CARL SANDBURG

THE KING

Old Tawny's mane is moth-
eaten now, a balding monk's tonsure
and his fluid thigh muscles flop
slack as an exhausted boxer's;

Creaks a little and is
just a fraction under fast (he's lame)
in those last short lethal rushes
at the slim white-eyed winging game;

Can catch them still of course,
the horny old claws combing crimson
from the velvet flanks in long scores,
here in the game-park's environs;

Each year, panting heavily,
manages with aged urbanity
to smile full-faced and yellowly
at a thousand box cameras.

DOUGLAS LIVINGSTONE

Once when the snow of the year was beginning to fall,
We stopped by a mountain pasture to say, 'Whose colt?'
A little Morgan had one forefoot on the wall,
The other curled at his breast. He dipped his head
And snorted at us. And then he had to bolt.
We heard the miniature thunder where he fled,
And saw him, or thought we saw him, dim and grey,
Like a shadow against the curtain of falling flakes.
'I think the little fellow's afraid of the snow.
He isn't winter-broken. It isn't play
With the little fellow at all. He's running away.
I doubt if even his mother could tell him, "Sakes,
It's only weather." He'd think she didn't know!
Where is his mother? He can't be out alone.'
And now he comes again with clatter of stone,
And mounts the wall again with whited eyes
And all his tail that isn't hair up straight.
He shudders his coat as if to throw off flies.
'Whoever it is that leaves him out so late,
When other creatures have gone to stall and bin,
Ought to be told to come and take him in.'

ROBERT FROST

THE EARLY PURGES

I was six when I first saw kittens drown.
Dan Taggart pitched them, 'the scraggy wee shits',
Into a bucket; a frail metal sound,

Soft paws scraping like mad. But their tiny din
Was soon soused. They were slung on the snout
Of the pump and the water pumped in.

'Sure isn't it better for them now?' Dan said.
Like wet gloves they bobbed and shone till he sluiced
Them out on the dunghill, glossy and dead.

Suddenly frightened, for days I sadly hung
Round the yard, watching the three sogged remains
Turn mealy and crisp as old summer dung

Until I forgot them. But the fear came back
When Dan trapped big rats, snared rabbits, shot crows
Or, with a sickening tug, pulled old hens' necks.

Still, living displaces false sentiments
And now, when shrill pups are prodded to drown
I just shrug, 'Bloody pups'. It makes sense:

'Prevention of cruelty' talk cuts ice in town
Where they consider death unnatural,
But on well-run farms pests have to be kept down.

SEAMUS HEANEY

— 5 —

I took my cat apart
to see what made him purr.
Like an electric clock
or like the snore

of a warming kettle,
something fizzled and sizzled in him.
Was he a soft car,
the engine bubbling sound?

Was there a wire beneath his fur,
or humming throttle?
I undid his throat.
Within was no stir.

I opened up his chest
as though it were a door:
no whisk or rattle there.
I lifted off his skull:

no hiss or murmur.
I halved his little belly
but found no gear,
no cause for static.

So I replaced his lid,
laced his little gut.
His heart into his vest I slid
and buttoned up his throat.

His tail rose to a rod
and beckoned to the air.
Some voltage made him vibrate
warmer than before.

Whiskers and a tail:
perhaps they caught
some radar code
emitted as a pip, a dot-and-dash

of woollen sound.
My cat a kind of tuning fork? –
amplifier? – telegraph? –
doing secret signal work?

His eyes elliptic tubes:
there's a message in his stare.
I stroke him
but cannot find the dial.

MAY SWENSON

— 6 —

THE MEADOW MOUSE

I

In a shoe box stuffed in an old nylon stocking
Sleeps the baby mouse I found in the meadow,
Where he trembled and shook beneath a stick
Till I caught him up by the tail and brought him in,
Cradled in my hand,
A little quaker, the whole body of him trembling,
His absurd whiskers sticking out like a cartoon-mouse,
His feet like small leaves,
Little lizard-feet,
Whitish and spread wide when he tried to struggle away,
Wriggling like a miniscule puppy.

Now he's eaten his three kinds of cheese and drunk from his
                              bottle-cap watering-trough —
So much he just lies in one corner,
His tail curled under him, his belly big
As his head; his bat-like ears
Twitching, tilting toward the least sound.

Do I imagine he no longer trembles
When I come close to him?
He seems no longer to tremble.

II

But this morning the shoe-box house on the back porch is empty.
Where has he gone, my meadow mouse,
My thumb of a child that nuzzled in my palm? —
To run under the hawk's wing,
Under the eye of the great owl watching from the elm-tree,
To live by courtesy of the shrike, the snake, the tom-cat.

I think of the nestling fallen into the deep grass,
The turtle gasping in the dusty rubble of the highway,
The paralytic stunned in the tub, and the water rising, —
All things innocent, hapless, forsaken.

THEODORE ROETHKE

THE RABBIT

(After Prévert)

We are going to see the rabbit.
We are going to see the rabbit.
Which rabbit, people say?
Which rabbit, ask the children?
Which rabbit?
The only rabbit.
The only rabbit in England,
Sitting behind a barbed-wire fence
Under the floodlights, neon lights,
Sodium lights,
Nibbling grass
On the only patch of grass
In England, in England
(Except the grass by the hoardings
Which doesn't count.)
We are going to see the rabbit.
And we must be there on time.

First we shall go by escalator,
Then we shall go by underground,
And then we shall go by motorway
And then by helicopterway,
And the last ten yards we shall have to go
On foot.

And now we are going
All the way to see the rabbit,
We are nearly there,
We are longing to see it,
And so is the crowd
Which is here in thousands
With mounted policemen
And big loudspeakers
And bands and banners,
And everyone has come a long way.
But soon we shall see it
Sitting and nibbling
The blades of grass
On the only patch of grass
In – but something has gone wrong!
Why is everyone so angry,
Why is everyone jostling
And slanging and complaining?

The rabbit has gone,
Yes, the rabbit has gone.
He has actually burrowed down into the earth
And made himself a warren, under the earth,
Despite all these people.
And what shall we do?
What *can* we do?

It is all a pity, you must be disappointed,
Go home and do something else for today,
Go home again, go home for today.
For you cannot hear the rabbit, under the earth,
Remarking rather sadly to himself, by himself,
As he rests in his warren, under the earth;
'It won't be long, they are bound to come,
They are bound to come and find me, even here.'

ALAN BROWNJOHN

IF THE OWL CALLS AGAIN

At dusk
from the island in the river,
and it's not too cold,

I'll wait for the moon
to rise,
then take wing and glide
to meet him.

We will not speak,
but hooded against the frost
soar above
the alder flats, searching
with tawny eyes.

And then we'll sit
in the shadowy spruce and
pick the bones
of careless mice,

while the long moon drifts
towards Asia
and the river mutters
in its icy bed.

And when morning climbs
the limbs
we'll part without a sound,
fulfilled, floating
homewards as
the cold world awakens.

JOHN HAINES

is my favourite. Who flies
like a nothing through the night,
who-whoing. Is a feather
duster in leafy corners ring-a-rosy-ing
boles of mice. Twice

you hear him call. Who
is he looking for? You hear
him hoovering over the floor
of the wood. O would you be gold
rings in the driving skull

if you could? Hooded and
vulnerable by the winter suns
owl looks. Is the grain of bark
in the dark. Round beaks are at
work in the pellety nest,

resting. Owl is an eye
in the barn. For a hole
in the trunk owl's blood
is to blame. Black talons in the
petrified fur! Cold walnut hands

on the case of the brain! In the reign
of the chicken owl comes like
a god. Is a goad in
the rain to the pink eyes,
dripping. For a meal in the day

flew, killed, on the moor. Six
mouths are the seed of his
arc in the season. Torn meat
from the sky. Owl lives
by the claws of his brain. On the branch

in the sever of the hand's
twigs owl is a backward look.
Flown wind in the skin. Fine
rain in the bones. Owl breaks
like the day. Am an owl, am an owl.

GEORGE MACBETH

Someone, perhaps a child, who is fascinated by owls creates a sort of spell to bring an owl into being. By the end of the poem he has become the owl.
G.M.

DEATH OF A BIRD

After those first days
When we had placed him in his iron cage
And made a space for him
    From such

Outrageous cage of wire,
Long and shallow, where the sunlight fell
Through the air, onto him;
    After

He had been fed for three days
Suddenly, in that sunlight before noon
He was dead with no
    Pretence.

He did not say goodbye
He did not say thankyou, but he died then
Lying flat on the rigid
    Wires

Of his cage, his gold
Beak shut tight, which once in hunger had
Opened as a trap
    And then

Swiftly closed again,
Swallowing quickly what I had given him;
How can I say I am sorry
    He died.

Seeing him lie there dead,
Death's friend with death, I was angry he
Had gone without pretext or warning,
    With no

Suggestion first he should go,
Since I had fed him, then put wires round him
Bade him hop across
    The bars of my hands.

I asked him only that
He should desire his life. He had become
Of us a black friend with
    A gold mouth

Shrilly singing through
The heat. The labour of the black bird! I
    Cannot understand why
        He is dead.

I bury him familiarly.
His heritage is a small brown garden.
Something is added to the everlasting earth;
From my mind a space is taken away.

JON SILKIN

PARROT

Sometimes I sit with both eyes closed,
But all the same, I've heard!
They're saying, 'He won't talk because
He is a *thinking* bird.'

I'm olive-green and sulky, and
The family say, 'Oh yes,
He's silent, but he's *listening*,
He *thinks* more than he *says*!

'He ponders on the things he hears,
Preferring not to chatter.'
– And this is true, but *why* it's true
Is quite another matter.

I'm working out some shocking things
In order to surprise them,
And when my thoughts are ready I'll
Certainly *not* disguise them!

I'll wait, and see, and choose a time
When everyone is present,
And clear my throat and raise my beak
And give a squawk and start to speak
And go on for about a week
And it will not be pleasant!

ALAN BROWNJOHN

A ROBIN

Ghost-grey the fall of night,
  Ice-bound the lane,
Lone in the dying light
  Flits he again;
Lurking where shadows steal,
Perched in his coat of blood,
Man's homestead at his heel,
  Death-still the wood.

Odd restless child; it's dark;
  All wings are flown
But this one wizard's – hark! –
  Stone clapped on stone!
Changeling and solitary,
Secret and sharp and small,
Flits he from tree to tree,
  Calling on all.

WALTER DE LA MARE

I ordered this, this clean wood box
Square as a chair and almost too heavy to lift.
I would say it was the coffin of a midget
Or a square baby
Were there not such a din in it.

The box is locked, it is dangerous.
I have to live with it overnight
And I can't keep away from it.
There are no windows, so I can't see what is in there.
There is only a little grid, no exit.

I put my eye to the grid.
It is dark, dark,
With the swarmy feeling of African hands
Minute and shrunk for export,
Black on black, angrily clambering.

How can I let them out?
It is the noise that appals me most of all,
The unintelligible syllables.
It is like a Roman mob,
Small, taken one by one, but my god, together!

I lay my ear to furious Latin.
I am not a Caesar.
I have simply ordered a box of maniacs.
They can be sent back.
They can die, I need feed them nothing, I am the owner.

I wonder how hungry they are.
I wonder if they would forget me
If I just undid the locks and stood back and turned into a tree.
There is the laburnum, its blond colonnades,
And the petticoats of the cherry.

They might ignore me immediately
In my moon suit and funeral veil.
I am no source of honey
So why should they turn on me?
Tomorrow I will be sweet God, I will set them free.

The box is only temporary.

SYLVIA PLATH

THE BEST BEAST OF ——— THE FAT-STOCK SHOW AT EARL'S COURT

(*In monosyllables*)

The Best Beast of the Show
Is fat,
He goes by the lift –
They all do that.

This lift, large as a room,
(Yet the beasts bunch),
Goes up with a groan,
They have not oiled the winch.

Not yet to the lift
Goes the Best Beast,
He has to walk on the floor to make a show
First.

Great are his horns,
Long his fur,
The Beast came from the North
To walk here.

Is he not fat?
Is he not fit?
Now in a crown he walks
To the lift.

When he lay in his pen,
In the close heat,
His head lolled, his eyes
Were not shut for sleep.

Slam the lift door,
Push it up with a groan,
Will they kill the Beast now?
Where has he gone?

When he lay in the straw
His heart beat so fast
His sides heaved, I touched his side
As I walked past.

I touched his side,
I touched the root of his horns;
The breath of the Beast
Came in low moans.

STEVIE SMITH

THE DISCLOSURE

From the shrivelling gray
silk of its cocoon
a creature slowly
        is pushing out
to stand clear —

                not a butterfly,
                    petal that floats at will across
                    the summer breeze
                not a furred
                moth of the night
                    crusted with indecipherable
                    gold —

some primal-shaped, plain-winged, day-flying thing.

DENISE LEVERTOV

TO THE SNAKE

Green Snake, when I hung you round my neck
and stroked your cold, pulsing throat
        as you hissed to me, glinting
arrowy gold scales, and I felt
        the weight of you on my shoulders,
and the whispering silver of your dryness
        sounded close at my ears —

Green Snake — I swore to my companions that certainly
        you were harmless! But truly
I had no certainty, and no hope, only desiring
        to hold you, for that joy,
                        which left
a long wake of pleasure, as the leaves moved
and you faded into the pattern
of grass and shadows, and I returned
smiling and haunted, to a dark morning.

DENISE LEVERTOV

A narrow Fellow in the Grass
Occasionally rides –
You may have met Him – did you not
His notice sudden is –

The Grass divides as with a Comb –
A spotted shaft is seen –
And then it closes at your feet
And opens further on –

He likes a Boggy Acre
A Floor too cool for Corn –
Yet when a Boy, and Barefoot –
I more than once at Noon
Have passed, I thought a Whip lash
Unbraiding in the Sun –
When stooping to secure it
It wrinkled, and was gone –

Several of Nature's People
I know, and they know me –
I feel for them a transport
Of cordiality –

But never met this Fellow
Attended, or alone
Without a tighter breathing
And Zero at the Bone –

EMILY DICKINSON

Workshop

Talking points

- What creatures have you kept as pets? What animals would you most like to keep? Why do people keep pets? (See 'Caring for Animals', p. 1.)

- Should we keep animals in captivity? Do you approve or disapprove of circuses? Hunting? Using animals for research? Zoos? (See 'The King', p. 3.)

- What responsibilities do we have towards animals? (See 'The Meadow Mouse', p. 7.) Can you ever 'own' a creature? (See 'The Early Purges, p. 5, and 'The Arrival of the Bee Box', p. 15.)

- What do you think of factory farming methods? Are we right to rear and kill animals for food? (See Stevie Smith's poem on p. 16.)

Drama

Some of the poems and pictures in this section might suggest situations and themes for improvisation. You might be able to develop something from the following brief ideas:

- Being in captivity – a caged animal? a prisoner in jail? a slave?

- Being hunted – a man on the run?

- Going to see the rabbit – a group improvisation based on Alan Brownjohn's poem on p. 8.

On p. 2, Carl Sandburg says: 'I got a zoo, I got a menagerie inside my ribs . . .' Look again at 'Wilderness' and see if you can find the creatures in yourself. Animal masks might help you.

Activity

MAKING A FOLDER OR DISPLAY

Collect together the following:

- some pictures of animals which you find particularly interesting – your own photographs or drawings, cut-outs from colour supplements, tracings from books;

- as much information as you can from library books and wildlife magazines about the animals shown in the pictures you have gathered;

- a short anthology of your own poems and stories, perhaps suggested by some of the animal poems and pictures in this book or by the pictures and information you have discovered for yourself.

Decide how to set out all this material. As a four-page magazine? A display to be put up on the wall of your classroom? Why not work in pairs or small groups?

You will also need sugar paper, plain and lined paper, tracing paper, glue, Sellotape and scissors.

Notebook

■ Observe your own pet closely and jot down your impressions of its appearance, behaviour and character.

■ Look closely at insect life on a patch of earth, on a window-pane or on a spider's web. Make notes, concentrating all the time on what the insects are *like*: what you are reminded of by what you see. From your notes, pick out images that appeal to you and try to work them into a poem of your own.

■ Sit quietly in a park or garden and concentrate on just one or two creatures and their surroundings – perhaps the ducks dreaming on the pond, the dog nosing its way about the undergrowth, the cat sitting, self-contained, on the wall, or the pigeons strutting importantly over the flagstones. Describe the creatures' appearance and how they move.

■ There may be a pond at your school or near your home where you can see frogs, fish, dragonflies, beetles, water boatmen and many other small creatures. Again, concentrate on one of these creatures and develop your own poem about it. Remember to use your senses. What does it *look* like? What would it *feel* like to touch? What does it *sound* like? And, in some cases, what does it *smell* like?

■ If there is a pet shop near your home, you could perhaps visit it and build up some notes on the sights, sounds and smells which help to create the atmosphere of the shop. Try to write your own poem based on what you have jotted down.

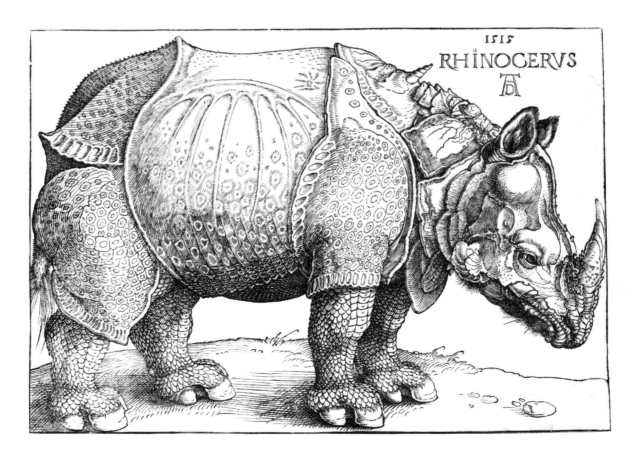

You

——— METAPHORS ———

I'm a riddle in nine syllables,
An elephant, a ponderous house,
A melon strolling on two tendrils.
O red fruit, ivory, fine timbers!
This loaf's big with its yeasty rising.
Money's new-minted in this fat purse.
I'm a means, a stage, a cow in calf.
I've eaten a bag of green apples,
Boarded the train there's no getting off.

SYLVIA PLATH

Love set you going like a fat gold watch.
The midwife slapped your footsoles, and your bald cry
Took its place among the elements.

Our voices echo, magnifying your arrival. New statue.
In a drafty museum, your nakedness
Shadows our safety. We stand round blankly as walls.

I'm no more your mother
Than the cloud that distils a mirror to reflect its own slow
Effacement at the wind's hand.

All night your moth-breath
Flickers among the flat pink roses. I wake to listen:
A far sea moves in my ear.

One cry, and I stumble from bed, cow-heavy and floral
In my Victorian nightgown.
Your mouth opens clean as a cat's. The window square

Whitens and swallows its dull stars. And now you try
Your handful of notes;
The clear vowels rise like balloons.

SYLVIA PLATH

BABY'S DRINKING SONG

*for a baby learning for the first time
to drink from a cup (Vivace)*

Sip a little
Sup a little
  From your little
Cup a little
  Sup a little
Sip a little
  Put it to your
Lip a little
  Tip a little
Tap a little
  Not into your
Lap or it'll
  Drip a little
Drop a little
  On the table
Top a little.

JAMES KIRKUP

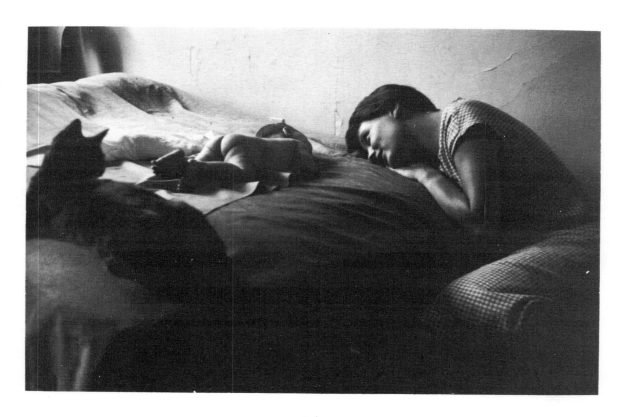

TO MY DAUGHTER

Bright clasp of her whole hand around my finger,
My daughter, as we walk together now.
All my life I'll feel a ring invisibly
Circle this bone with shining: when she is grown
Far from today as her eyes are far already.

STEPHEN SPENDER

AT SEVEN A SON

In cold weather on a
garden swing, his legs
in wellingtons rising over
the winter rose trees

he sits serenely
smiling like a Thai
his coat open, his gloves
sewn to the flapping sleeves

his thin knees working
with his arms
folded about the
metal struts

as he flies up
(his hair like long
black leaves) he
lies back freely

astonished in
sunshine as serious
as a stranger he is
a bird in his own thought.

ELAINE FEINSTEIN

A CHILD HALF-ASLEEP

Stealthily parting the small-hours silence,
a hardly-embodied figment of his brain
comes down to sit with me
as I work late.
Flat-footed, as though his legs and feet
were still asleep.

On a stool,
staring into the fire,
his dummy dangling.

Fire ignites the small coals of his eyes;
it stares back through the holes
into his head, into the darkness.

I ask what woke him.

'A wolf dreamed me,' he says.

TONY CONNOR

CHILDREN'S SONG

We live in our own world,
A world that is too small
For you to stoop and enter
Even on hands and knees,
The adult subterfuge.
And though you probe and pry
With analytic eye,
And eavesdrop all our talk
With an amused look,
You cannot find the centre
Where we dance, where we play,
Where life is still asleep
Under the closed flower,
Under the smooth shell
Of eggs in the cupped nest
That mock the faded blue
Of your remoter heaven.

R. S. THOMAS

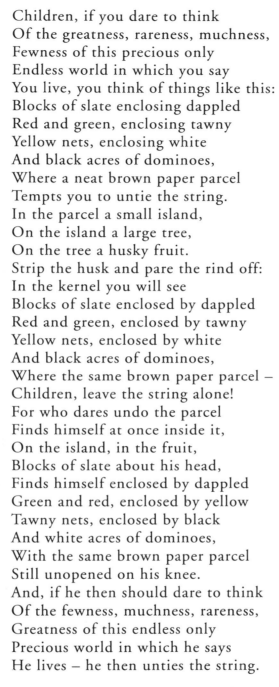

Children, if you dare to think
Of the greatness, rareness, muchness,
Fewness of this precious only
Endless world in which you say
You live, you think of things like this:
Blocks of slate enclosing dappled
Red and green, enclosing tawny
Yellow nets, enclosing white
And black acres of dominoes,
Where a neat brown paper parcel
Tempts you to untie the string.
In the parcel a small island,
On the island a large tree,
On the tree a husky fruit.
Strip the husk and pare the rind off:
In the kernel you will see
Blocks of slate enclosed by dappled
Red and green, enclosed by tawny
Yellow nets, enclosed by white
And black acres of dominoes,
Where the same brown paper parcel –
Children, leave the string alone!
For who dares undo the parcel
Finds himself at once inside it,
On the island, in the fruit,
Blocks of slate about his head,
Finds himself enclosed by dappled
Green and red, enclosed by yellow
Tawny nets, enclosed by black
And white acres of dominoes,
With the same brown paper parcel
Still unopened on his knee.
And, if he then should dare to think
Of the fewness, muchness, rareness,
Greatness of this endless only
Precious world in which he says
He lives – he then unties the string.

ROBERT GRAVES

Sam, Sam the dirty man,
Washed his face in a frying pan;
He combed his hair with a donkey's tail,
And scratched his belly with a big toe nail.
(general)

Oh my finger, oh my thumb,
Oh my belly, oh my bum.   (general)

Ladies and gentlemen
    Take my advice,
Pull down your pants
    And slide on the ice.   (general)

Isn't it funny, a rabbit's a bunny,
It has two ears, four legs; and a tummy.
(general)

An egg
A wee, wee hoose
Fou, fou o' meat,
Neither door nor window
To let you in to eat.

(Riddle: Kirkcaldy)

A lighted candle
Little Nancy Netticoat
Wears a white petticoat
The longer she lives
The shorter she grows,
Little Nancy Netticoat.

(Riddle: Shropshire)

I wet my finger,
I wipe it dry,
I cut my throat
If I tell a lie.

(Swearing truth: Lydney)

Same to you with knobs on,
Cabbages with clogs on,
Elephants with slippers on,
And you with dirty knickers on.

(Answering back: Lancashire)

Touch collar
Never swallow
Never get the fever,
Touch your nose
Touch your toes,
Never go in one of those.
         (To ward off ill luck on seeing
            an ambulance: Newcastle)

A duck in a pond,
A fish in a pool,
Whoever reads this
Is a big April fool.   (general)

While shepherds watched their turnip tops
    All boiling in the pot,
A lump of soot came rolling down
    And spoilt the bloomin' lot. (general)

We three kings of Orient are
One in a taxi, one in a car,
One on a scooter blowing his hooter
Following yonder star.   (general)

Mary had a little lamb,
    She also had a bear;
I've often seen her little lamb
    But I've never seen her *bear*.
                    (general)

In fourteen hundred and ninety-two
Columbus sailed the ocean blue;
He lost his yacht, the clumsy clot
That was a good one, was it not?
                    (general)

Splishy splashy custard, dead dogs' eyes,
All mixed up with giblet pies,
Spread it on the butty nice and thick
Swallow it down with a bucket of sick.
            (School dinners: Manchester)

Sir is kind and sir is gentle,
Sir is strong and sir is mental.

. . . No more Latin, no more French
No more sitting on a hard board bench
No more English, no more stick,
No more flipping arithmetic . . .
                (End of term: general)

(for Stephen)

Watch the net drift. Grey tides
Mingle what purposes your eye supposed
But watch the net. There is no fish
Only the net, the way it moves. There is no fish,
Forget the fish. The net is spread
And moving. Steer gently. Keep the hand
Pressured constantly against the stream.
There is no catch now, only the net
And your pressure and your poise. Below,
Ignore the pebbles and the promising weed
Mooning over its secrets. There is just the net,
The hand, and, now, near an old glance somewhere,
A sleek shape holding its body constant,
Firm in its fluid world. Move on. Watch
Only the net. You are a hand only,
Steering, controlling. Now look.
Inside that silent bulge the shape
Breaks black and firm. You may rise,
You may rise now – the deftest
Turn of wrist will do it. Your hand
Crude again can support the cling of mesh.
You can relax, coldly note
The titchy black squirm. You have achieved.
Commit success to jamjars. Lean again.
Dip the slack net. Let it belly.

BRIAN JONES

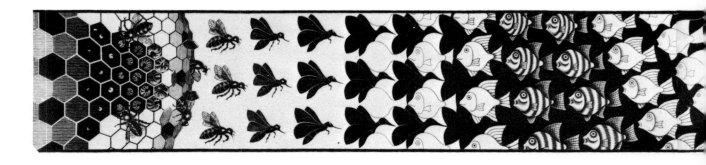

she sat down
at the scoured table
in the swept kitchen
beside the dresser with its cracked delft.
And every last crumb of daylight was salted away.

No one could say the stories were useless
for as the tongue clacked
five or forty fingers stitched
corn was grated from the husk
patchwork was pieced
or the darning done.

Never the one to slander her shiftless.
Daily sloven or spotless no matter whether
dishwater or tasty was her soup.
To tell the stories was her work.
It was like spinning,
gathering thin air to the singlest strongest
thread. Night in
she'd have us waiting, held
breath, for the ending we knew by heart.

And at first light
as the women stirred themselves to build the fire
as the peasant's feet felt for clogs
as thin grey washed over flat fields
the stories dissolved in the whorl of the ear
but they
hung themselves upside down
in the sleeping heads of the children
till they flew again
in the storytellers night.

LIZ LOCHHEAD

THE RAG DOLL TO
THE HEEDLESS CHILD

I love you
with my linen heart.

You cannot
know how these

rigid, lumpy arms
shudder in your grasp,

or what
tears dam up against

these blue eye-smudges at
your capriciousness.

At night I watch you sleep;
you'll never know

how I thrust my face
into the stream

of your warm breath;
and how

love-words choke me behind
this sewn-up mouth.

DAVID HARSENT

I have just hung my teddy bear.
I don't know why
Or what motives I had,
I just, hung him.
Before, he just lay there.
Stuffed and vile;
Seeing inside of me, and
Laughing.
Laughing at me, because I,
I was human.
That's why I hung him.
Because I was human,
But no longer;
I have hung him.
So he has won.

GRAHAM WALLEY

As I was going down Treak Street
For half a pound of treacle,
Who should I meet but my old friend Micky Thumps.
He said to me, 'Wilt thou come to our wake?'
I thought a bit,
I thought a bit,
I said I didn't mind;
So I went.

As I was sitting on our doorstep
Who should come by but my old friend Micky Thumps' brother.
He said to me, 'Wilt thou come to our house?
Micky is ill.'
I thought a bit,
I thought a bit,
I said I didn't mind:
So I went.

And he were ill:
He were gradely ill.
He said to me,
'Wilt thou come to my funeral, mon, if I die?'
I thought a bit,
I thought a bit,
I said I didn't mind:
So I went.

And it *were* a funeral.
Some stamped on his grave:
Some spat on his grave:
But I scraped my eyes out for my old friend Micky Thumps.

ANON

Who do you think you are
and where do you think you came from?
From toenails to the hair of your head you are
mixed of the earth, of the air,
Of compounds equal to the burning gold and ame-
thyst lights of the Mountains of the Blood of
Christ at Santa Fé.
Listen to the laboratory man tell what you are
made of, man, listen while he takes you apart.
Weighing 150 pounds you hold 3,500 cubic feet of
gas – oxygen, hydrogen, nitrogen.
From the 22 pounds and 10 ounces of carbon in
you is the filling for 9,000 lead pencils.
In your blood are 50 grains of iron and in the rest
of your frame enough iron to make a spike
that would hold your weight.
From your 50 ounces of phosphorous could be made
800,000 matches and elsewhere in your physical
premises are hidden 60 lumps of sugar, 20 tea-
spoons of salt, 38 quarts of water, two ounces
of lime, and scatterings of starch, chloride of
potash, magnesium, sulphur, hydrochloric acid.
You are a walking drug store and also a cosmos and
a phantasmagoria treading a lonesome valley,
one of the people, one of the minions and
myrmidons who would like an answer to the
question, 'Who and what are you?'
One of the people seeing sun, fog, zero weather,
seeing fire, flood, famine, having meditations
On fish, birds, leaves, seeds,
Skins and shells emptied of living form,
The beautiful legs of Kentucky thoroughbreds
And the patience of army mules.

CARL SANDBURG

THOUGHTS

Excuse me, isn't that you I see concealed underneath there
Inside the shield, or conning tower, of your head,
Your eyes looking out of the perforations in your flesh?
How can you think you can see from out of liquid, anyway?
     Are rain puddles watching me even now,
And can ducts which punctuate the underground of a field
Examine it at will for buried treasure? Is the rain outside your
     window a voyeur, then? Deep down under all that, though,
Underneath the liquids and the various unobservant stuffs
There is a spirit, shifting around from foot to foot.

MICHAEL BENEDIKT

THE CAULIFLOWER

I wanted to be a cauliflower,
all brain and ears,
thinking on the origin of gardens
and the divinity of him
who carefully binds my leaves.

With my blind roots touched
by the songs of the worms,
and my rough throat throbbing
with strange, vegetable sounds,
perhaps I'd feel the parting stroke
of a butterfly's wing . . .

Not like my cousins, the cabbages,
whose heads, tightly folded,
see and hear nothing of this world,
dreaming only on the yellow
and green magnificence
that is hardening within them.

JOHN HAINES

Mother,
       I won't be home this evening, so
don't worry; don't hurry to report me missing.
Don't drain the canals to find me,
I've decided to stay alive, don't
search the woods, I'm not hiding,
simply gone to get myself classified.
Don't leave my shreddies out,
I've done with security.
Don't circulate my photograph to society
I have disguised myself as a man
and am giving priority to obscurity.
It suits me fine;
I have taken off my short trousers
and put on long ones, and
now am going out into the city, so
don't worry; don't hurry to report me missing.

I've rented a room without any curtains
and sit behind the windows growing cold,
heard your plea on the radio this morning,
you sounded sad and strangely old. . . .

BRIAN PATTEN

This morning
 being rather young and foolish
 I borrowed a machine gun my father
 had left hidden since the war, went out
 and eliminated a number of small enemies.
 Since then I have not returned home.

This morning
 swarms of police with trackerdogs
 wander about the city
 with my description printed
 on their minds, asking:
 'Have you seen him?
 He is seven years old,
 likes Pluto, Mighty Mouse
 and Biffo the Bear,
 have you seen him, anywhere?'

This morning
 sitting alone in a strange playground
 muttering you've blundered, you've blundered
 over and over to myself
 I work out my next move
 but cannot move.
 The trackerdogs will sniff me out,
 they have my lollipops.

BRIAN PATTEN

FOR RUTH GAYLE CUNNINGHAM
*The twelfth grade at St Joseph's High School
in Jackson, Mississippi*

As I talk to these children hovering on the verge
Of man and woman, I remember the hanging back
Of my own fledgling, the alternate terror and joke
A child invokes, its claws frozen on the nest-edge.

Fly, I hear myself say now, though they're not my young,
And suddenly I see they are heavy as stones –
I see we are all of us heavy as stones –
How many years is it now I've been falling?

Then two of them, a thin, overbright white
Boy and a slower, steadier Negro girl,
Striking out, each make a fluttering whirl
And I know those two have already dreamt of the flight.

Oh, now the whole classroom is beating leaky wings
As if flying were a mere child's pantomime.
What a moment it is, what a mortal time –
Is there any plummet or flight as sheer as the fledgling's?

WILLIAM MEREDITH

DREAM OF THE CARDBOARD LOVER

She fell away from her earthly husband;
it was night in the city
and a dim lamp shone.

The street seemed empty and silent,
but on the pavement before her
lay something weakly flapping.

She bent over and saw in it
the shape of a man, but he
was flattened and thin like a carton.

She picked him up, and looking
into those battered eyes,
she thought she knew him, and cried:

'We sat together in school, long ago,
you were always the one I loved!'

And the cardboard hero shed a paper tear
as he leaned against her
in the dreamlight,
growing dimmer and dimmer.

JOHN HAINES

To fling my arms wide
In some place of the sun,
To whirl and to dance
Till the white day is done.
Then rest at cool evening
Beneath a tall tree
While night comes on gently,
    Dark like me –
That is my dream!

To fling my arms wide
In the face of the sun,

Dance! whirl! whirl!
Till the quick day is done
Rest at pale evening . . .
A tall, slim tree . . .
Night coming tenderly,
    Black like me.

LANGSTON HUGHES

IDYLL

I was drawing water from the well
When suddenly he looked at me –
I was so moved
That I let slip the rope.

TRADITIONAL AFRICAN

LOVE POEM

I live in you, you live in me;
We are two gardens haunted by each other.
Sometimes I cannot find you there,
There is only the swing creaking, that you have just left,
Or your favourite book beside the sundial.

DOUGLAS DUNN

I

When we talk, I imagine silence
Beyond the intervalling words: a space
Empty of all but ourselves there, face to face,
Away from others, alone in the intense
Light or dark, it would not matter which.

II

But where a room envelopes us, one heart,
Our bodies, locked together, prove apart
Unless we change them back again to speech.

III

Close to you here, looking at you, I see
Beyond your eyes looking back, that second you
Of whom the outward semblance is the image –
The inward being where the name springs true.

IV

Today, left only with a name, I rage,
Willing these lines – willing a name to be
Flesh, on the blank unanswering page.

STEPHEN SPENDER

VALENTINE

Not a red rose or a satin heart.

I give you an onion.
It is a moon wrapped in brown paper.
It promises light
like the careful undressing of love.

Here.
It will blind you with tears
like a lover.
It will make your reflection
a wobbling photo of grief.

I am trying to be truthful.

Not a cute card or a kissogram.

I give you an onion.
Its fierce kiss will stay on your lips,
possessive and faithful
as we are,
for as long as we are.

Take it.
Its platinum loops shrink to a wedding-ring,
if you like.
Lethal.
Its scent will cling to your fingers,
cling to your knife.

CAROL ANN DUFFY

When you visit Aunt Em you must whistle
Through railings, and her face will glide
Like a slow white moon to the window-space.

Then you must wait patiently
By the bruised door – (put your ear
Against it, you will hear how slow she comes).

When it opens, say with unusual breeziness
How are you then? but don't listen
For an answer. Instead, go down

Stairs murky as a lost century
And emerge in her underground cavern
Where a cat will panic in the darkness.

There, make as much noise as you can –
Hum, whistle, scrape a chair – before
She enters with that curious and catching malady

Of never having been or done anything.
While you stay, be on your guard.
She is a siren, although she weighs five stone

From some illness she has never recovered from,
Although her hair is thin and lank as a washing-up rag,
Although she keeps a finger crooked to stop a ring falling off.

Soon she will be capering for you, telling stories
Of how during the war she'd dive under the bed
So that the falling bomb would bounce back from the springs;

Of how the sole stripped from her shoe, and she walked
A mile sliding her foot to stop the cod's-mouth flap –
She flickers to life with visits: she forgets,

And soon you'll be groaning and wheezing, helpless.
But keep your wits about you; remember she
Is your kin. Haven't you seen somewhere

That paleness of eyes? that pallor of cheeks?
Haven't you known what it is to slump like that?
Isn't this cavern familiar? and the filtered daylight?

Wish her goodbye. Kiss her cheek as if it were lovely.
Thank her for the soft biscuits and the rancid butter.
Then straighten your tie, pull your cuffs square,

Think of tomorrow as a day when the real begins
With its time and teabreaks. Tell her you'll
Visit her again sometime, one quiet Sunday.

BRIAN JONES

—— LONG DISTANCE ——

Though my mother was already two years dead
Dad kept her slippers warming by the gas,
put hot water bottles her side of the bed
and still went to renew her transport pass.

You couldn't just drop in. You had to phone.
He'd put you off an hour to give him time
to clear away her things and look alone
as though his still raw love were such a crime.

He couldn't risk my blight of disbelief
though sure that very soon he'd hear her key
scrape in the rusted lock and end his grief.
He *knew* she'd just popped out to get the tea.

I believe life ends with death, and that is all.
You haven't both gone shopping; just the same,
in my new black leather phone book there's your name
and the disconnected number I still call.

TONY HARRISON

Crabbed Age and Youth
Cannot live together:
Youth is full of pleasance,
Age is full of care;
Youth like summer morn,
Age like winter weather;
Youth like summer brave,
Age like winter bare.
Youth is full of sport,
Age's breath is short;
Youth is nimble, Age is lame;
Youth is hot and bold,
Age is weak, and cold;
Youth is wild, and Age is tame.
Age, I do abhor thee;
Youth, I do adore thee;
O, my Love, my Love is young!
Age, I do defy thee:
O, sweet shepherd, hie thee!
For methinks thou stay'st too long.

WILLIAM SHAKESPEARE

Workshop

Talking points

In the group of poems and pictures in this section, we have tried to capture something of the process of growing up – from babyhood, through childhood and on to adolescence. Finally, in contrast, we have printed a few poems about old age.

■ What do you remember about your earliest years?

■ Which of you can go back furthest?

■ Does one incident stand out clearly and sharply in your memory?

■ Are there any similarities in the things each of you remembers? Are they sad or happy or frightening?

■ Can you distinguish what you were told by your parents from what *you* actually recall?

Share your memories by dividing up into small discussion groups.

Re-read Brian Jones' poem, 'Visiting Miss Emily' (p. 48), and Tony Harrison's poem, 'Long Distance' (p. 49), and discuss what pictures of old age each creates. How do the two poets see themselves in relation to old age? How do *you*?

Activities

PARENTS AND CHILDREN

Discussion
Browse through the poems about parents and young children on pp. 23–6 for a few minutes. Then spend some time as a class reading the poems out loud. Discuss both the poems and the pictures that accompany some of them.

A short piece of writing
After you have read the poems, choose the one you like best and write a paragraph or two saying what you like about it. You may want to include the thoughts and ideas the poem contains, the pictures it creates in your mind's eye, and any words, phrases or comparisons that appeal to you. Spend about twenty minutes on this.

Individual or group activities
As a follow-up piece of work, choose one of the activities below to work on by yourself or in a group:

■ Take one of the poems as a starting point for a piece of

drama. Childhood nightmares? New baby in the family? Family outing or disagreement?

- Write your own poem suggested by one of the poems or pictures in this section. Or find your own picture on the theme of parents and children and write about it. Present your work as a display or in folder form. Illustrate it with your own drawings or with a collage.

- Try to write a sequel to one of the poems, for example 'Father Half-Asleep' or 'Warning to Parents' or 'To My Mother'.

HOW TO ... WRITE A POEM?

Look at Brian Jones' poem 'How to Catch Tiddlers' on p. 32. Choose something practical that you know how to do and jot down some notes and ideas about it. Perhaps you could write your own poem explaining 'How to make ...' or 'How to Catch ...'

CHILDHOOD TOYS

The poems about childhood toys on pp. 34–5 may have reminded you of your own toys. They may still be around in a cupboard, or you may have handed them on to younger brothers or sisters. Perhaps you still (secretly?) cherish them, or maybe you can just dimly remember them. Choose your favourite toy and describe it in as much detail as you can, recording your feelings about it as you do so.

CHILDREN'S RHYMES

In their book *The Lore and Language of Schoolchildren* (published by Oxford University Press), Iona and Peter Opie have gathered together over 800 playground rhymes and chants, along with a vast amount of fascinating information about slang, riddles, jokes, nicknames and so on. Some of the more common rhymes are given on pp. 28–31 to jog your memory – in case you had forgotten.

What rhymes do you remember best?

- Skipping rhymes, 'dipping' rhymes, singing games, rhyming riddles?

- Rhymes about teachers, bigheads, cowards, crybabies, sneaks?

- Rhymes about the end of term, or ones said at a particular time of year, for example New Year, Christmas, 5 November, 1 April?

- Adaptations of popular songs, hymns or carols?

- Rhymes to tell you who you will marry or to prevent bad luck?

You will probably discover that you know many different ones, particularly if members of your class come from different parts of the country. Perhaps you could collect more from younger brothers and sisters and also from parents and grandparents. You could add to your store by listening to the youngest classes in your school when they play at break and lunchtime. Perhaps you could ask for permission to visit a local junior school to carry out some further research. You could make on-the-spot recordings with a tape recorder. As you learn more about this subject, you will find the Opies' book an invaluable guide.

The World Around You

Green Mistletoe!
Oh, I remember now
A dell of snow,
Frost on the bough;
None there but I:
Snow, snow, and a wintry sky.

None there but I,
And footprints one by one,
Zigzaggedly,
Where I had run;
Where shrill and powdery
A robin sat in the tree.

And he whistled sweet;
And I in the crusted snow
With snow-clubbed feet
Jigged to and fro,
Till, from the day,
The rose-light ebbed away.

And the robin flew
Into the air, the air,
The white mist through;
And small and rare
The night-frost fell
Into the calm and misty dell.

And the dusk gathered low,
And the silver moon and stars
On the frozen snow
Drew taper bars,
Kindled winking fires
In the hooded briers.

And the sprawling Bear
Growled deep in the sky;
And Orion's hair
Streamed sparkling by:
But the North sighed low,
'Snow, snow, more snow!'

WALTER DE LA MARE

Where fields and hollows were,
Ponds, lakes, and meres now stand.
From Warminster to Shaftesbury
The hills are icebergs in an arctic sea.
All's silent, livid, sour
As a sucked coin on the tongue.
The light's a gleam of blades,
Yet brackish; like an x-ray photograph's
Dark-grained dead world
It melts the skin off bone,
And reaching under tumuli
Becomes a hand, fine-fingered,
Bone of ivory and skin of wax,
That fondles dust.
                    High up,
Nude moon impassive as a fish's eye,
Has placed its watery mirrors here.
The stars have got their flicknives out.

A sentry, drawing breath, gulps
Nails of frost. The tanks are crouching
Under canvas hoods. Drowned settlements
As stark as tombs.
                    Across the road
A truck's upturned,
Its wheels responded to the icy kiss,
The bite now fastening in the driver's throat.
There's something in the pallor of his face,
Turned moonwards nervelessly,
Recalls a radiance
The sea was mad to have
When it laid first an image there,
Still groans about the world to keep
And on occasion gets,
To lie at dawn calm as a corpse.

JEREMY HOOKER

The man is clothed
in birchbark,
small birds cling to his limbs
and one builds
a nest in his ear.

The clamor of bedlam
infests his hair, a wind
blowing in his head
shakes down
a thought that turns
to moss and lichen
at his feet.

His eyes are blind
with April,
his breath distilled
of butterflies
and bees, and in his beard
the maggot sings.

He comes again
with litter of chips
and empty cans,
his shoes full of mud and dung;

an army of shedding dogs
attends him,
the valley shudders where
he stands,
             redolent of roses,
exalted in
the streaming rain.

JOHN HAINES

THAW

Suddenly air is careless, generous,
caressing where it gripped. On lawns
the snowmen shrink to tiny pyramids
their eyes of frizzled coke roll out like tears
the blackbird launches song on running streams
and rising like a tide the grass
wells over snow and leaves it islanded
while hills like withheld waves tremble to move.

Time lives again. There are ripples, rivulets
in lanes and gutters, shimmers across bark;
stones and jutting tree-roots shine, while
the heart that through the rigid months became
a memory of spring, an easy yearning,
must be itself again, trembling, susceptible.

BRIAN JONES

IN NATURE

Here too are life's victims,
captives of an old umbrella,
lives wrecked
by the lifting of a stone.

Sailors marooned
on the island of a leaf
when their ship
of mud and straw went down.

Explorers lost
among roots and raindrops,
drunkards sleeping it off
in the fields of pollen.

Cities of sand that fall,
dust towers that blow away.
Penal colonies
from which no one returns.

Here too, neighbourhoods
in revolt, revengeful columns;
evenings at the broken wall,
black armies in flight . . .

JOHN HAINES

Clouds

Sharp showers, bright between. Late in the afternoon, the light and shade being brilliant, snowy blocks of cloud were filing over the sky, and under the sun hanging above and along the earth-line were those multitudinous up-and-down crispy sparkling chains with pearly shadows up to the edges. At sunset, which was in a grey bank with moist gold dabs and racks, the whole round of skyline had level clouds naturally lead-colour but the upper parts ruddled, some more, some less, rosy. Spits or beams braided or built in with slanting pellet flakes made their way. Through such clouds anvil-shaped pink ones and up-blown fleece-of-wool flat-topped dangerous-looking pieces.

GERARD MANLEY HOPKINS

(From Journal Entry for 1 July 1866)

I watch a rock shine black
Behind thin water that falls with a frail sound
To the ferny pool. Elvers are roping upwards,
Tumultuous as hair. The rippling ground
Is elvers only, wriggling from crack to crack.

Above, a blackfaced ram,
Its viking head malevolent on the sky,
Peers down, stamps and is gone. A rowanberry
Skims and swims, a scarlet coracle, by.
Between two stones a grassblade breathes *I am*.

Small insect glitters run
On the water's skin ... I turn away and see
Distances looking over each other's shoulders
At a black cliff, a ferny pool and me
And a tress of elvers rippling in the sun.

NORMAN MacCAIG

From: WEATHER BESTIARY

Sun

A hard summer. The month I sat at the rock
One fish rose, belly up, a dead gleam.

Thunder

Corn, lobster, fleece hotly harvested – now
That whale stranded on the blue rock!

Frost

Stiff windless flower, hearse-blossom,
Show us the brightness of blood, stars, apples.

Fog

The sun-dipped isle was suddenly a sheep
Lost and stupid, a dense wet tremulous fleece.

Snow

Autumn, a moulted parrot, eyes with terror
This weird white cat. It drifts the rose-bush under.

GEORGE MACKAY BROWN

Snow in January
Looking for ledges
To hide in unmelted.

February evening:
A cold puddle of petrol
Makes its own rainbow.

Wind in March:
No leaves left
For its stiff summons.

April sunlight:
Even the livid bricks
Muted a little.

Wasp in May
Storing his venom
For a long summer.

Morning in June:
On the sea's horizon
A white island, alone.

July evening:
Sour reek of beer
Warm by the river.

August morning:
A squirrel leaps and
Only one branch moves.

September chestnuts:
Falling too early,
Split white before birth.

October garden:
At the top of the tree
A thrush stabs an apple.

November morning:
A whiff of cordite
Caught in the leaf mould.

Sun in December:
In his box of straw
The tortoise wakes.

ANTHONY THWAITE

Day after day
the withered reeds break off
and drift away.

RANKO

(*Trans. H. G. Henderson*)

I've found a small dragon in the woodshed.
Think it must have come from deep inside a forest
because it's damp and green and leaves
are still reflecting in its eyes.

I fed it on many things, tried grass,
the roots of stars, hazel-nut and dandelion,
but it stared up at me as if to say, I need
food you can't provide.

It made a nest among the coal,
not unlike a bird's but larger,
it is out of place here
and is quite silent.

If you believed in it I would come
hurrying to your house to let you share my wonder,
but I want instead to see
if you yourself will pass this way.

BRIAN PATTEN

OBSERVATION

Now and then concentrating
on the very small,

focusing my attention
on a very small area

like this crack in sandstone
perpetually wet with seepage,

getting so close
to moss, liverwort and fern

it becomes a forest
with wild beasts in it,

birds in the branches
and crickets piping,

cicadas shrilling.
Someone seeing me

staring so fixedly
at nothing

might be excused
for thinking me vague, abstracted,

lost in introspection.
No! I am awake, absorbed,

just looking in a different direction.

W. HART-SMITH

Sunday morning

       and the sun
       bawls
       with
       his big mouth

Yachts

       paper triangles
       of white and blue
       crowd the sloping bay
       appearing motionless
       as if stuck there
       by some infant thumb

       beneath a shouting sky

       upon a painted sea

WES MAGEE

In a salt ring of moonlight
The dinghy nods at nothing.
It paws the bright water
And scatters its own shadow
In a false net of light.

A ruined chain lies reptile,
Tied to the ground by grasses.
Two oars, wet with sweet water
Filched from the air, are slanted
From a wrecked lobster creel.

The cork that can't be travels –
Nose of a dog otter.
It's piped at, screamed at, sworn at
By elegant oyster catcher
On furious red legs.

With a sort of idle swaying
The tide breathes in. Harsh seaweed
Uncrackles to its kissing;
The skin of the water glistens;
Rich fat swims on the brine.

And all night in his stable
The dinghy paws bright water,
Restless steeplechaser
Longing to clear the hurdles
That ring the Point of Stoer.

NORMAN MacCAIG

To step over the low wall that divides
Road from concrete walk above the shore
Brings sharply back something known long before –
The miniature gaiety of seasides.
Everything crowds under the low horizon:
Steep beach, blue water, towels, red bathing caps,
The small hushed waves' repeated fresh collapse
Up the warm yellow sand, and further off
A white steamer stuck in the afternoon –

Still going on, all of it, still going on!
To lie, eat, sleep in hearing of the surf
(Ears to transistors, that sound tame enough
Under the sky), or gently up and down
Lead the uncertain children, frilled in white
And grasping at enormous air, or wheel
The rigid old along for them to feel
A final summer, plainly still occurs
As half an annual pleasure, half a rite,

As when, happy at being on my own,
I searched the sand for Famous Cricketers,
Or, farther back, my parents, listeners
To the same seaside quack, first became known.
Strange to it now, I watch the cloudless scene:
The same clear water over smoothed pebbles,
The distant bathers' weak protesting trebles
Down at its edge, and then the cheap cigars,
The chocolate-papers, tea-leaves, and, between

The rocks, the rusting soup-tins, till the first
Few families start the trek back to the cars.
The white steamer has gone. Like breathed-on glass
The sunlight has turned milky. If the worst
Of flawless weather is our falling short,
It may be that through habit these do best,
Coming to water clumsily undressed
Yearly; teaching their children by a sort
Of clowning; helping the old, too, as they ought.

PHILIP LARKIN

THE BONFIRE

Day by day, day after day, we fed it
With straw, mown grass, shavings, shaken weeds,
The huge flat leaves of umbrella plants, old spoil
Left by the builders, combustible; yet it
Coughed fitfully at the touch of a match,
Flared briefly, spat flame through a few dry seeds
Like a chain of fireworks, then slumped back to the soil
Smouldering and smoky, leaving us to watch

Only a heavy grey mantle without fire.
This glum construction seemed choked at heart,
The coils of newspaper burrowed into its hulk
Led our small flames into the middle of nowhere,
Never touching its centre, sodden with rot.
Ritual petrol sprinklings wouldn't make it start
But swerved and vanished over its squat brown bulk,
Still heavily sullen, grimly determined not

To do away with itself. A whiff of smoke
Hung over it as over a volcano.
Until one night, late, when we heard outside
A crackling roar, and saw the far field look
Like a Gehenna* claiming its due dead.   *hell
The beacon beckoned, fierily aglow
With days of waiting, hiding deep inside
Its bided time, ravenous to be fed.

ANTHONY THWAITE

I RETURN TO THE PLACE I WAS BORN

From my youth up I never liked the city.
I never forgot the mountains where I was born.
The world caught me and harnessed me
And drove me through dust, thirty years away from home.
Migratory birds return to the same tree.
Fish find their way back to the pools where they were hatched.
I have been over the whole country,
And have come back at last to the garden of my childhood.
My farm is only ten acres.
The farm house has eight or nine rooms.
Elms and willows shade the back garden.
Peach trees stand by the front door.
The village is out of sight.
You can hear dogs bark in the alleys,
And cocks crow in the mulberry trees.
When you come through the gate into the court
You will find no dust or mess.
Peace and quiet live in every room.
I am contented to stay here the rest of my life.
At last I have found myself.

T'AO YUAN MING

(*Trans. K. Rexroth*)

ON ROOFS OF TERRY STREET

Television aerials, Chinese characters
In the lower sky, wave gently in the smoke.

Nest-building sparrows peck at moss,
Urban flora and fauna, soft, unscrupulous.

Rain drying on the slates shines sometimes.
A builder is repairing someone's leaking roof,

He kneels upright to rest his back,
His trowel catches the light and becomes precious.

DOUGLAS DUNN

I asked directions
at a farmhouse door:
they pointed to a field
high on the hillside
where they said
the Giant's Grave
stood, and waited,
watching by their gate,
an old man
and his wife, watching
till I turned the road,
wondering perhaps why
a man would climb
half a mountain to see
a heap of stones.

Over the ditch and through
the rising bog spotted
with tiny spits of wild cotton
I moved, a mile
an hour, until the land
below became a mood,
long shadows sweeping
inland, eating light . . .

Armed with bright pictures
of club and claw
I searched until suddenly
it grinned at me:
filling the hole in a crazy hedge
it overflowed into the field –
great tables impaled
upon a pencil of stone;
a tabernacle of ancient death
dug deep as an evil eye
in the skull of the hill.
I banished urgent images
from my downward path and one
by one unclenched
the stone cold fingers round my brain.

RICHARD RYAN

The night rattles with nightmares.
Children cry in the close-packed houses,
A man rots in his snoring.
On quiet feet, policemen test doors.
Footsteps become people under streetlamps.
Drunks return from parties,
Sounding of empty bottles and old songs.
The young women come home,
The pleasure in them deafens me.
They trot like small horses
And disappear into white beds
At the edge of the night.
All windows open, this hot night,
And the sleepless, smoking in the dark,
Making small red lights at their mouths,
Count the years of their marriages.

DOUGLAS DUNN

HOTEL ROOM, 12TH FLOOR

This morning I watched from here
a helicopter skirting like a damaged insect
the Empire State Building, that
jumbo size dentist's drill, and landing
on the roof of the PanAm skyscraper.
But now midnight has come in
from foreign places. Its uncivilised darkness
is shot at by a million lit windows, all
ups and acrosses.

But midnight is not
so easily defeated. I lie in bed, between
a radio and a television set, and hear
the wildest of warwhoops continually ululating through
the glittering canyons and gulches –
police cars and ambulances racing
to the broken bones, the harsh screaming
from coldwater flats, the blood
glazed on sidewalks.

The frontier is never
somewhere else. And no stockades
can keep the midnight out.

NORMAN MACCAIG

Into the world of the red glass bus
came a man with a face like a hippopotamus

Grotesqueeruptions made horrific
an otherwise normal ugly face
Wartsscrambled over his head
peeping between thin twigs of dry hair
like pink shiny sunsets
Hanging below the neckline
like grapes festering on a vine
And when he blinked
you could glimpse the drunken dance
in the whites of his eyes
like the flash of underpants
through unbuttoned trouserflies

Had the passengers been in groups
there might have been laughter
But they were all singles
and turning their faces to the windows
did not see the view
but behind the privacy of eyelids
had a mental spew

Limpinggropingly looking for a place
went the substandard man
with the hunchbacked face
and finding one sat
and beholding his mudstudded boots
the hippopotamusman
wondered whether it was wednesday.

ROGER McGOUGH

Excuse me
standing on one leg
I'm half-caste

Explain yuself
wha yu mean
when yu say half-caste
yu mean when picasso
mix red an green
is a half-caste canvas/
explain yuself
wha yu mean
when yu say half-caste
yu mean when light an shadow
mix in de sky
is a half-caste weather/
well in dat case
england weather
nearly always half-caste
in fact some o dem cloud
half-caste till dem overcast
so spiteful dem dont want de sun pass
ah rass/
explain yuself
wha yu mean
when yu say half-caste
yu mean tchaikovsky
sit down at dah piano
an mix a black key
wid a white key
is a half-caste symphony/

Explain yuself
wha yu mean
Ah listening to yu wid de keen
half of mih ear
Ah lookin at yu wid de keen
half of mih eye
an when I'm introduced to yu
I'm sure you'll understand
why I offer yu half-a-hand
an when I sleep at night
I close half-a-eye
consequently when I dream
I dream half-a-dream
an when moon begin to glow
I half-caste human being
cast half-a-shadow
but yu must come back tomorrow

wid de whole of yu eye
an de whole of yu ear
an de whole of yu mind

an I will tell yu
de other half
of my story

JOHN AGARD

CHECKING OUT ME HISTORY

Dem tell me
Dem tell me
Wha dem want fo tell me

Bandage up me eye with me own history
Blind me to me own identity

Dem tell me bout 1066 and all dat
Dem tell me bout Dick Whittington and he cat
But Toussaint L'Ouverture[1]
no dem never tell me bout dat

Toussaint
a slave
with vision
lick back
Napoleon
battalion
and first Black

Republic born
Toussaint de thorn
to de French
Toussaint de beacon
of de Haitian Revolution
Dem tell me bout de man who discover de balloon
and de cow who jump over de moon

Dem tell me bout de dish run away with de spoon
but dem never tell me bout Nanny de maroon[2]

Nanny
see-far woman
of mountain dream
fire-woman struggle
hopeful stream
to freedom river

[1] rarely mentioned in school history books. A slave who led an army that defeated forces sent by Napoleon
[2] a national heroine of Jamaica. She led runaway slaves to establish a free colony in the hills of Jamaica

Dem tell me bout Lord Nelson and Waterloo
but dem never tell me bout Shaka de great Zulu
Dem tell me bout Columbus and 1492
but what happen to de Caribs[3] and de Arawaks too

Dem tell me bout Florence Nightingale and she lamp
and how Robin Hood used to camp
Dem tell me bout old King Cole was a merry ole soul
but dem never tell me bout Mary Seacole[4]

From Jamaica
she travel far
to the Crimean War
she volunteer to go
and even when de British said no
she still brave the Russian snow
a healing star
among the wounded
a yellow sunrise
to the dying

Dem tell me
Dem tell me wha dem want fo tell me
By now I checking out me own history
I carving out me identity.

JOHN AGARD

[3] Amerindian tribe from whom the Caribbean got its name
[4] the Jamaican nurse who put her skills to use in the Crimean War (1853–6) but who did not receive the acclaim that Florence Nightingale did

Landlord, landlord,
My roof has sprung a leak.
Don't you 'member I told you about it
Way last week?

Landlord, landlord,
These steps is broken down.
When you come up yourself
It's a wonder you don't fall down.

Ten bucks you say I owe you?
Ten bucks you say is due?
Well, that's ten bucks more'n I'll pay you
Till you fix this house up new.

What? You gonna get eviction orders?
You gonna cut off my heat?
You gonna take my furniture and
Throw it in the street?

Um-huh! You talking high and mighty.
Talk on – till you get through.
You ain't gonna be able to say a word
If I land my fist on you.

Police! Police!
Come and get this man!
He's trying to ruin the government
And overturn the land!

Copper's whistle!
Patrol bell!
Arrest.

Precinct station.
Iron cell.
Headlines in press:

Man threatens landlord

Tenant held no bail

Judge gives Negro 90 days in county jail

LANGSTON HUGHES

THE GIRL-CHILD OF POMPEI

Since everyone's anguish is our own,
We live yours over again, thin child,
Clutching your mother convulsively
As though, when the noon sky turned black,
You wanted to re-enter her.
To no avail, because the air, turned poison,
Filtered to find you through the closed windows
Of your quiet thick-walled house,
Once happy with your song, your timid laugh.
Centuries have passed, the ash has petrified
To imprison those delicate limbs for ever.
In this way you stay with us, a twisted plaster cast,
Agony without end, terrible witness to how much
Our proud seed matters to the gods.
Nothing is left of your far-removed sister,
The Dutch girl imprisoned by four walls
Who wrote of her youth without tomorrows.
Her silent ash was scattered by the wind,
Her brief life shut into a crumpled notebook.
Nothing remains of the Hiroshima schoolgirl,
A shadow printed on a wall by the light of a thousand suns,
Victim sacrificed on the altar of fear.
Powerful of the earth, masters of new poisons,
Sad secret guardians of final thunder,
The torments heaven sends us are enough.
Before your finger presses down, stop and consider.

20 NOVEMBER 1978

PRIMO LEVI

(Trans. Ruth Feldman and Brian Swann)

Workshop

Discussion and writing

THE SEASONS

On pp. 54–8, there are poems and pictures about different seasons and times of the year. What is your favourite time of year? Quickly jot down some of the things that make it so. You could begin each line with the same phrase, for example: 'What I like about summer is . . .', and make a list poem which ends: 'But best of all is the. . . .'

Or you could choose to reverse the idea and write: 'What I *hate* about winter is . . .', and end: 'But *worst* of all. . . .'

If enough of you are able to contribute lines that you all like, you could build up a set of class poems – one for each of the four seasons – and perhaps illustrate them.

Anthony Thwaite's poem on p. 59 is composed of twelve haiku poems. A haiku is a Japanese verse form which is ideally, though not necessarily, composed of seventeen syllables arranged over three lines in the pattern 5, 7, 5. Try to write your own haiku sequence for the year, concentrating on producing four verses, one for each season. You may find that you can pull out four of the best ideas from the class poems (above) as starting points.

LOOKING AND SEEING

Much of the writing in this section depends on close observation of the natural world for its effect. Gerard Manley Hopkins' observation of clouds, which he wrote in his journal or diary (p. 57), shows us a writer jotting down the rough, impressionistic material which he might later work up into a poem. Similarly, the poem 'Observation' on p. 62 shows us a writer absorbed in the tiny world he sees in a small fissure in a rock, looking inwards with the mind's eye rather than outwards.

Choose a natural feature or object on which you can focus your attention. It might be the cloudscape outside the window; the trees across the way; the fine detail of the palm of your hand; the complexity of somebody's eye. Using comparisons, try to jot down images that will help the reader see what you see, feel what you feel.

PLACES

Richard Ryan's poem, 'A Heap of Stones' (p. 68), tells of a visit to a lonely prehistoric stone burial place in the hills. There is something frightening about the atmosphere of the place. Do you know a place which has the power to frighten you – perhaps when you were younger? What's the loneliest place you can remember? Perhaps a moorland? A deserted beach? A street late at night? Maybe you felt lonely when you were out in a small boat or when you were swimming away from the shore? Talk about the experience and see if you have the basis for a piece of writing.

'I Return to the Place I was Born' (p. 67). Returning to a place after a long absence can be an unsettling experience. Sometimes it is because things *are* very different: the area has been bulldozed, and new houses and shops have been built, for example. Sometimes the place has stayed the same, but things we remember from early childhood seem so much *smaller* now we are older.

Have you ever returned to a place where you once lived, or to a previous school, or to somewhere you visited years ago on holiday? Were things as you remembered them? Had the place changed, or had you? Share your ideas, focus on your particular experiences and then try to write about your feelings.

Shapes

watch the words
watch words the
watchword is
watch words are   away.
sly as boots
ifyoutakeyoureyesoffthemforaminute

               they're   up   and

                              allover

                     the

                       place

ROGER McGOUGH

```
generation upon
generation upon
generation upon
generation upon
generation upon
generation upon
generation upon
generation upon
generation upon
generation upon
generation upon
generation upon
generation upon
generation upon
generation upon
generation upon
generation upon
generation upon
g  neration upon
g  neration up  n
g  nerat on up  n
g  nerat   n up  n
g  nerat   n  p  n
g   erat   n  p  n
g   era    n  p  n
g   era    n     n
g   er     n     n
g    r     n     n
g          n     n.
g          n
g
```

EDWIN MORGAN

THE FAN

Slowly, slowly
I unfold and Oh! what mysteries I behold:
with flowers and leaves my pattern
weaves and many creepers festoon
my trees. Beneath the amber wastes
of sky a loaded ox-cart trundles
by: the weary peasants wend
their way against the pale
of dying day. Gently
now I close again,
l i k e   w a v e s
r e c e d i n g
w h e n c e
they
c
a
m
e.

MALCOLM TIMPERLEY

UPON HIS DEPARTURE HENCE

Thus I
Passe by,
And die:
As One,
Unknown,
And gon:
I'm made
A shade,
And laid
I'th grave,
There have
My Cave.
Where tell
I dwell,
Farewell.

ROBERT HERRICK

George Herbert wrote this pattern poem nearly four hundred years ago, shortly before his death. The printer had no instructions as to how the two verses should appear on the page and therefore turned them sideways (the effect you get if you turn this book through 90 degrees). Traditionally, they have been printed that way ever since.

However, Professor David West, assisted by the calligrapher Rachel West (whose reproduction of an early manuscript version of the poem is shown below), argues convincingly for the verses to be printed as you see them here. The shape does not, he claims, represent angels' wings, as the old printed version suggested, but rather the wings of two larks flying across the sky from left to right. And they are flying eastwards for Easter, hence the careful ending of each line with the letter 'e'. The two verses also represent the two high points of Easter – the Crucifixion ('thy sacrifice') and the Resurrection ('thy victorie').

The argument of the poem as described by Professor West is that Man was created in plenty in the Garden of Eden but, through his folly, his resources have shrunk, as does the poem. As the poem swells again, Herbert prays to be able to rise with God. The further he has fallen, the further he will fly. The second stanza has a similar run of sense, but ends with a metaphor from falconry. If a falcon damages its wing, feathers can be taken from another falcon and grafted – *imped* – into place. Herbert imagines his own puny wings grafted like feathers into the mighty wings of God.

Easter Wings

Lord who createdst man in wealth and store
Though foolishly he lost the same
Decaying more and more
Till he became
Most poore
With thee
O let mee rise
As larks do by degree
And sing this day thy sacrifice
Then shall my fall further the flight in mee

Easter Wings

My tender age in sorrow did beginne
Yet thou with sicknesses and shame
Dayly dost punish sinne
Till I became
Most thinne
With thee
Lett mee combine
And feel thy victorie
For if I impe my wing on thine
Affliction shall advance the flight in mee

This Crosse-Tree here
Doth JESUS *beare,*
Who sweet'ned first,
The Death accurs't.
Here all things ready are, make hast, make hast away;
For, long this work wil be, & very short this Day.
Why then, go on to act: Here's wonders to be done,
Before the last least sand of Thy ninth houre be run;
Or e're dark Clouds do dull, or dead the Mid-dayes Sun.

Act when Thou wilt,
Bloud will be spilt;
Pure Balm, that shall
Bring Health to All.
Why then, Begin
To powre first in
Some Drops of Wine,
In stead of Brine,
To search the Wound,
So long unsound:
And, when that's done,
Let Oyle, next, run,
To cure the Sore
Sinne made before.
And O! Deare Christ,
E'en as Thou di'st,
Look down, and see
Us weepe for Thee.
And tho (Love knows)
Thy dreadfull Woes
Wee cannot ease;
Yet doe Thou please,
Who Mercie art,
T'accept each Heart,
That gladly would
Helpe, if it could.
Meane while, let mee,
Beneath this Tree,
This Honour have,
To make my grave.

ROBERT HERRICK

here's a little mouse)and
what does he think about, i
wonder as over this
floor(quietly with

bright eyes)drifts(nobody
can tell because
Nobody knows, or why
jerks Here &, here,
gr(oo)ving the room's Silence)this like
a littlest
poem a
(with wee ears and see?

tail frisks)

                    (gonE)

'mouse',
          We are not the same you and

i, since here's a little he
or is
it It
?   (or was something we saw in the mirror)?

therefore we'll kiss; for maybe
what was Disappeared
into ourselves
who   (look).   ,startled

                              e. e. cummings

ALAN RIDDELL

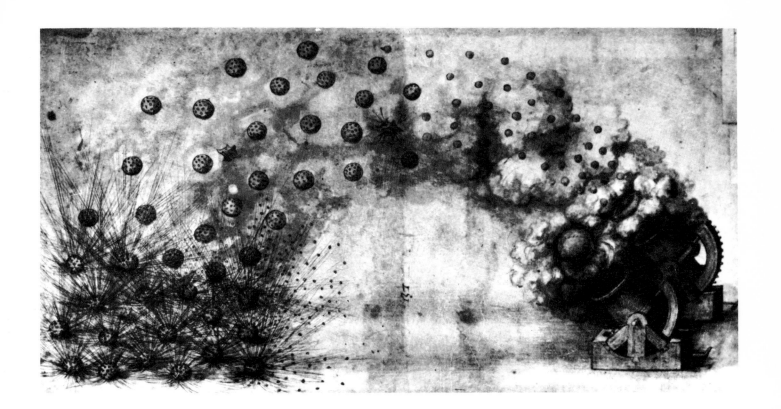

HEART AND MIRROR

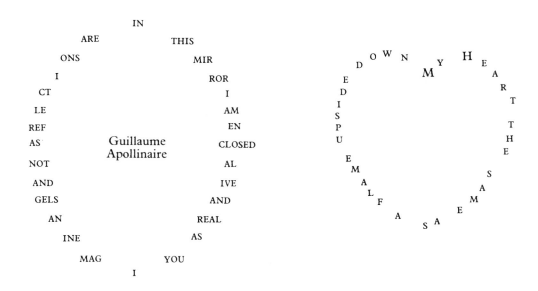

The left calligram (mirror shape) reads:

```
                IN
        ARE           THIS
    ONS                   MIR
    I                         ROR
    CT                        I
    LE                        AM
    REF                       EN
    AS      Guillaume         CLOSED
    NOT     Apollinaire       AL
    AND                       IVE
    GELS                      AND
      AN                    REAL
        INE               AS
          MAG         YOU
              I
```

The right calligram (heart shape) reads:

```
              D  O  W  N
           E                 M Y   H
           D                         E
           I                          A
           S                          R
           P                          T
           U                          
             E                      H
               M                  E
                 A              M
                  L          E
                     F    A
                        S  A
```

GUILLAUME APOLLINAIRE

Workshop

Talking points

- How do you react to the shape poems in this section? Are they fun? Irritating? Gimmicky? Thoughtful attempts at making a design with words? Substitutes for rhyme and metre?

- Could any of these poems be printed normally, without losing anything? Does the shape actually help you to understand the poem in each case?

Experiments

Take some everyday object – your wristwatch, a pair of compasses, an elastic band, a ring, a coin, a piece of string, your hand itself – and try to write something brief but apt about the object you choose *in the shape of the object*. It might be helpful to sketch an outline of the object first.

Now try starting with words and see what shapes they suggest or dictate. In each case, think about the sound of the word and the associations it has for you in your mind's eye. Try these:

bee	oily	veins	rocks
branches	forked	blot	cloud

Some of these words will not suggest any picture to you, let alone a particular shape, but try to work on one of them (or another word of your choice) by drawing the outline it brings to mind and writing a description inside the outline.

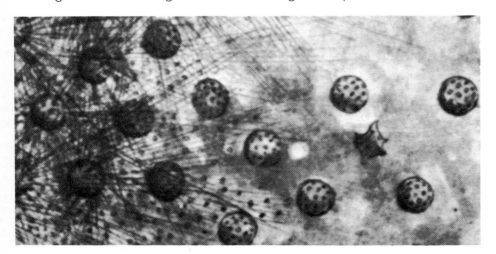

Activities

Try to write some shape poems, using either pencil and paper or a computer. One might have different line lengths to represent a silhouette of the subject of the poem on the page, as in 'Fan' (p. 82) and 'Easter Wings' (p. 83).

Another might be set out like Apollinaire's poems on p. 87, as though the letters were the actual lines of a drawing.

Or you may want to try a 'concrete' poem like 'Archives' (p. 81) or 'Revolver' (p. 86) where the layout is more important than the meaning of the words in the poem.

Once you have made your two-dimensional poems, try to turn them into three-dimensional ones. With some help from the Art department, you can spend a very enjoyable (and surprisingly difficult) lesson, making 3-D shapes and structures from your shape poems. Some might be suitable for use as mobiles or as classroom decorations.

Trace the Leonardo picture on p. 87 and construct a shape poem, like Alan Riddell's poem 'Revolver' (p. 86), by arranging words, letters, ideas and comparisons inside your tracing.

Songs

--- **LITTLE BOXES** ---

Little boxes on the hillside, little boxes made of ticky-tacky,
Little boxes, little boxes, little boxes all the same;
There's a green one and a pink one and a blue one and a yellow one,
And they're all made out of ticky-tacky
And they all look just the same.

And the people in the houses all go to the university,
And they all get put in boxes, little boxes, all the same;
And there's doctors and there's lawyers and business executives,
And they're all made out of ticky-tacky
And they all look just the same.

And they all play on the golf course and drink their martini dry,
And they all have pretty children and the children go to school;
And the children go to summer camp and then to the university,
And they all get put in boxes
And they all come out the same.

And the boys go into business and marry and raise a family,
And they all get put in boxes, little boxes, all the same;
There's a green one and a pink one and a blue one and a yellow one,
And they're all made out of ticky-tacky
And they all look just the same.

M. REYNOLDS

(*Sung by Pete Seeger*)

Picture yourself in a boat on a river,
With tangerine trees and marmalade skies;
Somebody calls you, you answer quite slowly,
A girl with kaleidoscope eyes.
Cellophane flowers of yellow and green,
Towering over your head.
Look for the girl with the sun in her eyes,
And she's gone.
Lucy in the sky with diamonds.
Follow her down to a bridge by a fountain
Where rocking horse people eat marshmallow pies,
Everyone smiles as you drift past the flowers,
That grow so incredibly high.
Newspaper taxis appear on the shore,
Waiting to take you away.
Climb in the back with your head in the clouds,
And you're gone.
Lucy in the sky with diamonds.
Picture yourself on a train in a station,
With plasticine porters with looking glass ties,
Suddenly someone is there at the turnstile,
The girl with kaleidoscope eyes.

JOHN LENNON and PAUL McCARTNEY

(*Sung by The Beatles on* Sgt. Pepper)

Wednesday morning at five o'clock as the day begins,
Silently closing her bedroom door,
Leaving the note that she hoped would say more,
She goes downstairs to the kitchen clutching her handkerchief;
Quietly turning the backdoor key,
Stepping outside she is free.
She (We gave her most of our lives)
is leaving (Sacrificed most of our lives)
home (We gave her everything money could buy).
She's leaving home after living alone
For so many years. Bye-bye.
Father snores as his wife gets into her dressing gown,
Picks up the letter that's lying there,
Standing alone at the top of the stairs
She breaks down and cries to her husband,
'Daddy, our baby's gone.
Why would she treat us so thoughtlessly?
How could she do this to me?'
She (We never thought of ourselves)
is leaving (Never a thought for ourselves)
home (We struggled hard all our lives to get by).
She's leaving home after living alone
For so many years. Bye-bye.
Friday morning at nine o'clock she is far away,
Waiting to keep the appointment she made,
Meeting a man from the motor trade.
She (What did we do that was wrong?)
is having (We didn't know it was wrong)
fun (Fun is the one thing that money can't buy).
Something inside that was always denied
For so many years. Bye-bye.
She's leaving home. Bye-bye.

JOHN LENNON and PAUL McCARTNEY

(*Sung by The Beatles on* Sgt. Pepper)

When I get older losing my hair,
Many years from now,
Will you still be sending me a Valentine,
Birthday greetings bottle of wine?
If I'd been out till quarter to three
Would you lock the door?
Will you still need me, will you still feed me,
When I'm sixty-four?
You'll be older too,
And if you say the word,
I could stay with you.
I could be handy, mending a fuse
When your lights have gone.
You can knit a sweater by the fireside,
Sunday morning go for a ride;
Doing the garden, digging the weeds,
Who could ask for more?
Will you still need me, will you still feed me,
When I'm sixty-four?
Every summer we can rent a cottage
In the Isle of Wight, if it's not too dear.
We shall scrimp and save;
Grandchildren on your knee,
Vera, Chuck and Dave.
Send me a postcard, drop me a line,
Stating point of view;
Indicate precisely what you mean to say
Yours sincerely, wasting away.
Give me your answer, fill in a form,
Mine for evermore;
Will you still need me, will you still feed me,
When I'm sixty-four?

JOHN LENNON and PAUL MCCARTNEY

(*Sung by The Beatles on* Sgt. Pepper)

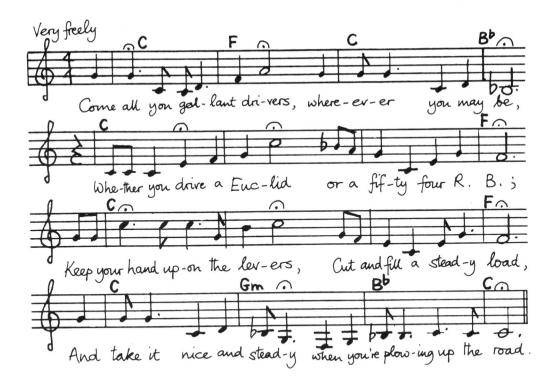

Very freely

Come all you gal-lant dri-vers, where-ev-er you may be,
Whe-ther you drive a Euc-lid or a fif-ty four R. B.;
Keep your hand up-on the lev-ers, Cut and fill a stead-y load,
And take it nice and stead-y when you're plow-ing up the road.

We've dug a hundred air fields, in the snow
    and wind and rain,
Built atomic power stations, more dams
    than I can name,
We've dug through rock and swampland,
    moved mountains by the load,
Now we're going nice and steady, boys,
    a-plowing up the road.

When your digging days are over and you've
    loaded your last ton,
When your *cat* is broken up for scrap and
    your ten R. B. won't run,
When you've had your last stamp on your
    card and reached your last abode,
For a long time after there'll be people
    travelling on your road.

EWAN MacCOLL

When you're weary, feeling small,
When tears are in your eyes, I will dry them all;
I'm on your side. When times get rough
And friends just can't be found,
Like a bridge over troubled water
I will lay me down.
Like a bridge over troubled water
I will lay me down.

When you're down and out,
When you're on the street,
When evening falls so hard
I will comfort you.
I'll take your part.
When darkness comes
And pain is all around,
Like a bridge over troubled water
I will lay me down.
Like a bridge over troubled water
I will lay me down.

Sail on silvergirl,
Sail on by.
Your time has come to shine.
All your dreams are on their way.
See how they shine.
If you need a friend
I'm sailing right behind.
Like a bridge over troubled water
I will ease your mind.
Like a bridge over troubled water
I will ease your mind.

PAUL SIMON

(Sung by Simon and Garfunkel)

One love, one heart.
Let's get together and feel all right.
Hear the children crying. (One love.)
Hear the children crying. (One heart.)
Sayin', 'Give thanks and praise to the Lord
    and I will feel all right.'
Sayin', 'Let's get together and feel all right,'
Whoa, whoa, whoa, whoa.

Let them all pass all their dirty remarks.
    (One love.)
There is one question I'd really love to ask.
    (One heart.)
Is there a place for the hopeless sinner
Who has hurt all mankind just to save his own?
Believe me.

One love, one heart.
Let's get together and feel all right.
As it was in the beginning. (One love.)
So shall it be in the end. (One heart.)
All right, 'Give thanks and praise to the Lord
    and I will feel all right.'
'Let's get together and feel all right.'
One more thing.

Let's get together to fight this Holy
    Armageddon, (One love.)
So when the Man comes there will be no,
    no doom. (One song.)
Have pity on those whose chances grow thinner.
There ain't no hiding place from the Father of
    Creation.

Sayin', 'One love, one heart.
Let's get together and feel all right.'
I'm pleading to mankind. (One love.)
Oh Lord. (One heart.) Whoa.

'Give thanks and praise to the Lord
    and I will feel all right.'
Let's get together and feel all right.
(Repeat)

BOB MARLEY (Sung on *Legend*)

Last night I heard the screaming,
Loud voices behind the wall,
Another sleepless night for me,
It won't do no good to call the police,
Always come late if they come at all.

And when they arrive,
They say they can't interfere with domestic affairs,
Between a man and his wife,
And as they walk out the door,
The tears well up in her eyes.

Last night I heard the screaming,
Then a silence that chilled my soul,
I prayed that I was dreaming when I saw the ambulance in the road,
And the policeman said,
'I'm here to keep the peace,
Will the crowd disperse,
I think we all could use some sleep.'

TRACY CHAPMAN (Sung on *Tracy Chapman*)

Workshop

Discussion and writing

Every time you listen to the lyric of a song, you are listening to a poem. Some songs have less 'substance' to them than others and may be little more than rhythmic repetitions of the same phrase – good for dancing and atmosphere, but not very interesting when printed on the page.

Some singers/songwriters are rather more concerned with what they have to say. In this section, we have printed a number of folk and pop lyrics that at different times have appealed to us or to our classes. One of the great appeals of pop music is that it changes continually and goes through fashions, though we believe that there are a number of very good pop lyrics that are likely to last. For example, some of the Beatles' songs have already been around for over thirty years; many even older songs have been re-recorded in modern versions by contemporary singers. The less commercial folk songs of Ewan MacColl may not be well known to you, but the best of them stand as poems in their own right.

Our suggestion is that you should read the lyrics in this section, talk about them as poems and, where possible, listen to recordings of them. Do some appeal more than others? Do your parents have favourite songs that date back to the time when they were your age? Can you find the words? What do you think of the lyrics and music?

GROUP WORK

Now, if you were to compile your own collection of lyrics that seem to you to have something to say, which ones would you include from the songs that have appeared in the past eighteen months? Each member of the group could suggest one or two songs and copy out the lyrics. Then each group could make up a mini-anthology to share, both as words on the page and as songs to be listened to.

Eight Poets

SYLVIA PLATH

Sylvia Plath took her own life in London in 1963 at the age of 30. She was born in Boston, Massachusetts, and educated in the United States, graduating from Smith College in 1955. She came to Britain immediately afterwards to study at Cambridge for the next two years, during which time she met and married the poet Ted Hughes. All of her work was crowded into the short period between her graduation and her death, most of her poems being written in the last three or four years of her life.

Certain poems and lines of poetry seem as solid and miraculous to me as church altars or the coronation of queens must seem to people who revere quite different images. I am not worried that poems reach relatively few people. As it is, they go surprisingly far – among strangers, around the world, even. Farther than the words of the classroom teacher or the prescriptions of a doctor; if they are very lucky, farther than a lifetime.

(From 'Context' by Sylvia Plath in *The London Magazine*, February 1962)

Overnight, very
Whitely, discreetly,
Very quietly

Our toes, our noses
Take hold on the loam,
Acquire the air.

Nobody sees us,
Stops us, betrays us;
The small grains make room.

Soft fists insist on
Heaving the needles,
The leafy bedding,

Even the paving.
Our hammers, our rams,
Earless and eyeless,

Perfectly voiceless,
Widen the crannies,
Shoulder through holes. We

Diet on water,
On crumbs of shadow,
Bland-mannered, asking

Little or nothing.
So many of us!
So many of us!

We are shelves, we are
Tables, we are meek,
We are edible,

Nudgers and shovers
In spite of ourselves.
Our kind multiplies:

We shall by morning
Inherit the earth.
Our foot's in the door.

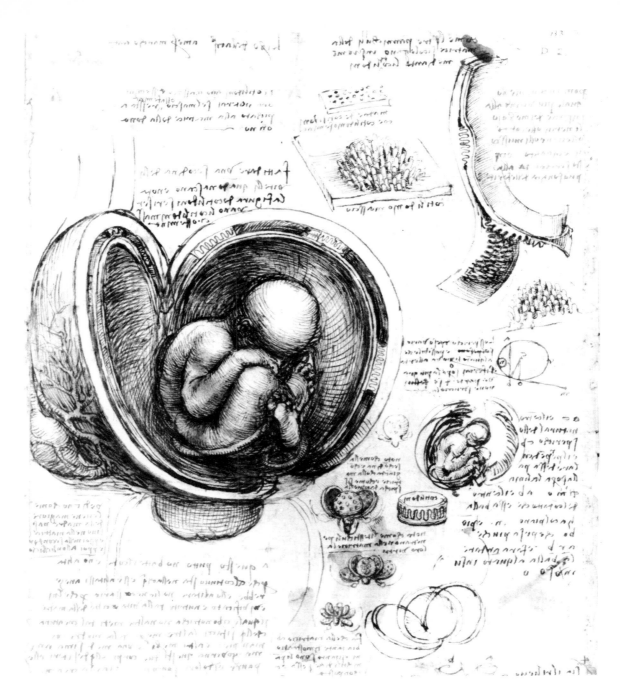

——— You're ———

Clownlike, happiest on your hands,
Feet to the stars, and moon-skulled,
Gilled like a fish. A common-sense
Thumbs-down on the dodo's mode.
Wrapped up in yourself like a spool,
Trawling your dark as owls do.
Mute as a turnip from the Fourth
Of July to All Fools' Day,
O high-riser, my little loaf.

Vague as fog and looked for like mail.
Farther off than Australia.
Bent-backed Atlas, our travelled prawn.
Snug as a bud and at home
Like a sprat in a pickle jug.
A creel of eels, all ripples.
Jumpy as a Mexican bean.
Right, like a well-done sum.
A clean slate, with your own face on.

Since Christmas they have lived with us,
Guileless and clear,
Oval soul-animals,
Taking up half the space,
Moving and rubbing on the silk

Invisible air drifts,
Giving a shriek and pop
When attacked, then scooting to rest, barely trembling.
Yellow cathead, blue fish —
Such queer moons we live with

Instead of dead furniture!
Straw mats, white walls
And these travelling
Globes of thin air, red, green,
Delighting

The heart like wishes or free
Peacocks blessing
Old ground with a feather
Beaten in starry metals.
Your small

Brother is making
His balloon squeak like a cat.
Seeming to see
A funny pink world he might eat on the other side of it,
He bites,

Then sits
Back, fat jug
Contemplating a world clear as water.
A red
Shred in his little fist.

At this wharf there are no grand landings to speak of.
Red and orange barges list and blister
Shackled to the dock, outmoded, gaudy,
And apparently indestructible.
The sea pulses under a skin of oil.

A gull holds his pose on a shanty ridgepole,
Riding the tide of the wind, steady
As wood and formal, in a jacket of ashes,
The whole flat harbour anchored in
The round of his yellow eye-button.

A blimp swims up like a day-moon or tin
Cigar over his rink of fishes.
The prospect is dull as an old etching.
They are unloading three barrels of little crabs.
The pier pilings seem about to collapse

And with them that rickety edifice
Of warehouses, derricks, smokestacks and bridges
In the distance. All around us the water slips
And gossips in its loose vernacular,
Ferrying the smells of dead cod and tar.

Farther out, the waves will be mouthing icecakes –
A poor month for park-sleepers and lovers.
Even our shadows are blue with cold.
We wanted to see the sun come up
And are met, instead, by this iceribbed ship,

Bearded and blown, an albatross of frost,
Relic of tough weather, every winch and stay
Encased in a glassy pellicle.
The sun will diminish it soon enough:
Each wave-tip glitters like a knife.

I am silver and exact. I have no preconceptions.
Whatever I see I swallow immediately
Just as it is, unmisted by love or dislike.
I am not cruel, only truthful –
The eye of a little god, four-cornered.
Most of the time I meditate on the opposite wall.
It is pink, with speckles. I have looked at it so long
I think it is a part of my heart. But it flickers.
Faces and darkness separate us over and over.

Now I am a lake. A woman bends over me,
Searching my reaches for what she really is.
Then she turns to those liars, the candles or the moon.
I see her back, and reflect it faithfully.
She rewards me with tears and an agitation of hands.
I am important to her. She comes and goes.
Each morning it is her face that replaces the darkness.
In me she has drowned a young girl, and in me an old woman
Rises toward her day after day, like a terrible fish.

U. A. FANTHORPE

U. A. Fanthorpe has described herself as 'a middle-aged drop-out'. Born in London in 1929, she was educated at Oxford and then taught at Cheltenham Ladies' College where she was later Head of the English Department. Her first volume of poetry did not appear until 1978. Since then, she has been able to devote more time to her writing and produced several further volumes for the Peterloo Press.

Her subjects range widely, from some memorable poems written in response to paintings (especially 'Not My Best Side' about Uccello's *St George and the Dragon*: see also *Double Vision*, pp. 32–33), to poems which draw on her knowledge of school (as in the first two printed here), and those which focus on the hospital work in which she was engaged for many years. Her tone of voice is often wryly humorous as she catches the characteristic behaviour of young and old ('Half-past Two' and 'Costa Geriatrica'), or as she sets 'the record straight' about the story of Lazarus ('Unauthorised Version').

Once upon a schooltime
He did Something Very Wrong
(I forget what it was).

And She said he'd done
Something Very Wrong, and must
Stay in the school-room till half-past two.

(Being cross, she'd forgotten
She hadn't taught him Time.
He was too scared of being wicked to remind her.)

He knew a lot of time: he knew
Gettinguptime, timeyouwereofftime,
Timetogohomenowtime, TVtime,

Timeformykisstime (that was Grantime).
All the important times he knew,
But not half-past two.

He knew the clockface, the little eyes
And two long legs for walking,
But he couldn't click its language,

So he waited, beyond onceupona,
Out of reach of all the timefors,
And knew he'd escaped for ever

Into the smell of old chrysanthemums on Her desk,
Into the silent noise his hangnail made,
Into the air outside the window, into ever.

And then, *My goodness*, she said,
Scuttling in, *I forgot all about you.*
Run along or you'll be late.

So she slotted him back into schooltime,
And he got home in time for teatime,
Nexttime, notimeforthatnowtime,

But he never forgot how once by not knowing time,
He escaped into the lockless land of ever,
Where time hides tick-less waiting to be born.

SPECIAL

We were special, our class.
Others knew less than us
(More, sometimes), but we were us,
The Clerks of the Weather,
Miss Knowles said.

We knew long words for him,
Our Weather, and had little toys
Like bones for dogs. Weather likes
Pinecones and seaweed,
So we brought them for him
(Or her). When they've decided if
It's boy-weather or girl-weather,
Miss Knowles will tell us,
She said.

Nice thing about Weather is
He knows what he's going to do
Before he does it, and *we* know
What *he* knows. That's why we're special.

I think of him, our Weather, shaggy old dog,
Lying all hairy by the fire of the sun,
Then barking, and shaking snow all over the world,
Or breathing fog at us, sending loony messages
In seaweed and fircones. *Good* dog, Weather.
I'll have a dog just like you when I grow up.

I wasn't good
At being a baby. Burrowed my way
Through the long yawn of infancy,
Masking by instinct how much I knew
Of the senior world, sabotaging
As far as I could, biding my time,
Biting my rattle, my brother (in private),
Shoplifting daintily into my pram.
Not a good baby,
No.

I wasn't good
At being a child. I missed
The innocent age. Children,
Being childish, were beneath me.
Adults I despised or distrusted. They
Would label my every disclosure
Precocious, naïve, whatever it was.
I disdained definition, preferred to be surly.
Not a nice child,
No.

I wasn't good
At adolescence. There was a dance,
A catchy rhythm; I was out of step.
My body capered, nudging me
With hairy, fleshy growths and monthly outbursts,
To join the party. I tried to annul
The future, pretended I knew it already,
Was caught bloody-thighed, a criminal
Guilty of puberty.
Not a nice girl,
No.

(My hero, intransigent Emily,
Cauterized her own-dog-mauled
Arm with a poker,
Struggled to die on her feet,
Never told anyone anything.)

I wasn't good
At growing up. Never learned
The natives' art of life. Conversation
Disintegrated as I touched it,
So I played mute, wormed along years,
Reciting the hard-learned arcane litany
Of cliché, my company passport.
Not a nice person,
No.

The gift remains
Masonic, dark. But age affords
A vocation even for wallflowers.
Called to be connoisseur, I collect,
Admire, the effortless bravura
Of other people's lives, proper and comely,
Treading the measure, shopping, chaffing,
Quarrelling, drinking, not knowing
How right they are, or how, like well-oiled bolts,
Swiftly and sweet, they slot into the grooves
Their ancestors smoothed out along the grain.

Evening quarters; land
Of the tranquil solo deckchair,
Of the early Ovaltine nightcap.

Here patient shop-assistants
Pick the right change from freckled
Trembling hands, and wrap

Single rashers tenderly. Here gardening
Is dangerous as bull-fights.
Dogs are dwarfish,

Coddled and lethal.
Here sagas are recited
Of long-dead husbands,

Varicose veins, comforting ministers,
Scarcity of large-print library books,
And endless hands of photographs

Of the happily-ever-after children
They make believe they have:
A nice son in the police force

And two lovely children.
Marriages are made in heaven,
For Mr Right not only exists

But arrives on cue. Tragedy
Is reduced to a foot-note. *The husband?*
Oh, he went wrong, or died,

Or something. They have all
Had what they wanted:
A lovely little square family,

And now, comforting morticians:
That's the man I want at my funeral,
If anything ever happens to me.

— 111 —

BC:AD

This was the moment when Before
Turned into After, and the future's
Uninvented timekeepers presented arms.

This was the moment when nothing
Happened. Only dull peace
Sprawled boringly over the earth.

This was the moment when even energetic Romans
Could find nothing better to do
Than counting heads in remote provinces.

And this was the moment
When a few farm workers and three
Members of an obscure Persian sect

Walked haphazard by starlight straight
Into the kingdom of heaven.

UNAUTHORISED VERSION

(for Elma Mitchell)

'Martha was cumbered about much serving, and came to him, and said Lord, does thou not care that my sister hath left me to serve alone? bid her therefore that she help me. And Jesus answered and said unto her, Martha, Martha, thou art careful and troubled about many things: but one thing is needful: and Mary hath chosen that good part.'

St Luke 10, vss 38–42

Of course he meant it kindly. I know that.
I know Josh – as well as anyone can know
The Son of God. All the same, he slipped up
Over this one. After all, a Son is only a son
When you come to think about it. And this
Was between sisters. Marty and me,
We understand each other. For instance, when Lazzie died,
We didn't need to spell it out between us,
Just knew how to fix the scenario
So Josh could do his bit – raising Lazzie, I mean,
From the dead. He has his own way of doing things,
Has to muddle people first, so then the miracle
Comes as a miracle. If he'd just walked in
When Lazzie was ill, and said *OK, Lazzie,*
You're off the sick list now – that'd have lacked *impact.*

But all this weeping, and groaning, and moving of stones,
And praying in public, and Mart saying *I believe etcetera,*
Then *Lazarus, come forth!* and out comes Lazzie
In his shroud. Well, even a halfwit could see
Something out of the ordinary was going on.
But this *was* just ordinary. A lot of company,
A lot of hungry men, not many helpers,
And Mart had a go at me in front of Josh,
Saying *I'm all on my own out there. Can't you*
Tell that sister of mine to take her finger out,
And lend a hand? Well, the thing about men is,
They don't realise how *temperamental* good cooks are.
And Mart is very good. Believe you me.
She was just blowing her top. No harm in it.
I knew that. But then Josh gives her
This monumental dressing-down, and really,
It wasn't fair. The trouble with theology is, it features
Too much miraculous catering. Those ravens feeding Elijah,
For instance. I ask you! They'd have been far more likely
To *eat* him. And all those heaven-sent fast-food take-aways –
Quail, and manna, and that. And Josh himself –
The famous fish-butty picnic, and that miraculous
Draught of fishes. What poor old Mart could have done with
Was a miraculous draught of coffee and sandwiches
Instead of a ticking-off. And the men weren't much help.
Not a *thank you* among them, and never a thought
Of help with the washing-up.

Don't get me wrong. Of course I love Josh,
Wonder, admire, believe. He knows I do.
But to give Marty such a rocket
As if she was a Pharisee, or that sort of type,
The ones he has it in for. It wasn't right.
Still, Josh himself, as I said – well, he *is* only
The Son of God, not the Daughter; so how could he know?
And when it comes to the truth, I'm Marty's sister.
I was there; I heard what was said, and
I knew what was meant. The men will write it up later
From their angle, of course. But this is me, Mary,
Setting the record straight.

GILLIAN CLARKE

Gillian Clarke was born in Cardiff in 1937 and educated at the
University there. After a short time working for the BBC in London,
she returned to Wales in 1960, and has lived and worked there ever since. She
published her first poems in the 1970s and her work became more widely
known with *Letter From a Far Country* (1982). The long title poem was
commissioned by the BBC as a half-hour radio poem and takes the form of a
letter from a fictitious woman to men in general. It is both a feminist protest and
a celebration of the rich details of local Welsh life.

Many of Gillian Clarke's poems combine a sense of the contribution women
make to society with a clear eye for personal, domestic details. The tone may be
reflective ('My Box'), or bitter-sweet ('Overheard in County Sligo'); the occasion
may be a poetry reading ('Miracle on St David's Day'), or the effects of the
Chernobyl disaster in 1986 ('Neighbours'). In all these poems she relates local
details to a more general awareness of the values by which people live.

My box is made of golden oak,
my lover's gift to me.
He fitted hinges and a lock
of brass and a bright key.
He made it out of winter nights,
sanded and oiled and planed,
engraved inside the heavy lid
in brass, a golden tree.

In my box are twelve black books
where I have written down
how we have sanded, oiled and planed,
planted a garden, built a wall,
seen jays and goldcrests, rare red kites,
found the wild heartsease, drilled a well,
harvested apples and words and days
and planted a golden tree.

On an open shelf I keep my box.
Its key is in the lock.
I leave it there for you to read,
or them, when we are dead,
how everything is slowly made,
how slowly things made me,
a tree, a lover, words, a box,
books and a golden tree.

'They flash upon that inward eye
Which is the bliss of solitude'
'The Daffodils' by W. Wordsworth

An afternoon yellow and open-mouthed
with daffodils. The sun treads the path
among cedars and enormous oaks.
It might be a country house, guests strolling,
the rumps of gardeners between nursery shrubs.

I am reading poetry to the insane.
An old woman, interrupting, offers
as many buckets of coal as I need.
A beautiful chestnut-haired boy listens
entirely absorbed. A schizophrenic

on a good day, they tell me later.
In a cage of first March sun a woman
sits not listening, not seeing, not feeling.
In her neat clothes the woman is absent.
A big, mild man is tenderly led

to his chair. He has never spoken.
His labourer's hands on his knees, he rocks
gently to the rhythms of the poems.
I read to their presences, absences,
to the big, dumb labouring man as he rocks.

He is suddenly standing, silently,
huge and mild, but I feel afraid. Like slow
movement of spring water or the first bird
of the year in the breaking darkness,
the labourer's voice recites 'The Daffodils'.

The nurses are frozen, alert; the patients
seem to listen. He is hoarse but word-perfect.
Outside the daffodils are still as wax,
a thousand, ten thousand, their syllables
unspoken, their creams and yellows still.

Forty years ago, in a Valleys school,
the class recited poetry by rote.
Since the dumbness of misery fell
he has remembered there was a music
of speech and that once he had something to say.

When he's done, before the applause, we observe
the flowers' silence. A thrush sings
and the daffodils are flame.

I married a man from County Roscommon
and I live at the back of beyond
with a field of cows and a yard of hens
and six white geese on the pond.

At my door's a square of yellow corn
caught up by its corners and shaken,
and the road runs down through the open gate
and freedom's there for the taking.

I had thought to work on the Abbey stage
or have my name in a book,
to see my thought on the printed page,
or still the crowd with a look.

But I turn to fold the breakfast cloth
and to polish the lustre and brass,
to order and dust the tumbled rooms
and find my face in the glass.

I ought to feel I'm a happy woman
for I lie in the lap of the land,
and I married a man from County Roscommon
and I live at the back of beyond.

STORM

The cat lies low, too scared
to cross the garden.

For two days we are bowed
by a whiplash of hurricane.

The hill's a wind-harp.
Our bones are flutes of ice.

The heart drums in its small room
and the river rattles its pebbles.

Thistlefields are comb and paper
whisperings of syllable and bone

till no word's left
but thud and rumble of

something with hooves or wheels,
something breathing too hard.

FEBRUARY

Lamb-grief in the fields
and a cold as hard as slate.
Foot and hoof are shod

with ice. Our footprints
seem as old as ferns in stone.
Air rings in ash and thorn.

Ice on the rain-butt, thick
as a shield and the tap chokes,
its thumb in its throat.

The stream runs black
in a ruff of ice, its caught breath
furls a frieze of air.

At night ice sings
to the strum of my thrown stones
like a snapped harp-string.

The pond's glass eye holds
leaf, reed, fish, paperweight
in a dream of stone

NEIGHBOURS

That spring was late. We watched the sky
and studied charts for shouldering isobars.
Birds were late to pair. Crows drank from the lamb's eye.

Over Finland small birds fell: song-thrushes
steering north, smudged signatures on light,
migrating warblers, nightingales.

Wing-beats failed over fjords, each lung a sip of gall.
Children were warned of their dangerous beauty.
Milk was spilt in Poland. Each quarrel

the blowback from some old story,
a mouthful of bitter air from the Ukraine
brought by the wind out of its box of sorrows.

This spring a lamb sips caesium on a Welsh hill.
A child, lifting her face to drink the rain,
takes into her blood the poisoned arrow.

Now we are all neighbourly, each little town
in Europe twinned to Chernobyl, each heart
with the burnt fireman, the child on the Moscow train.

In the democracy of the virus and the toxin
we wait. We watch for bird migrations,
one bird returning with green in its voice,

glasnost,
golau glas,*   *blue light
a first break of blue.

(MOS-14) KOPELOVO STATE FARM, U.S.S.R., May 11 (AP)—FALLOUT WARN
young girl at the Kopelovo State Farm Friday stands by a sign listing prec
against fallout from the Chernobyl atomic power station. These include a
to limit children's playtime outside and to beware of dust on leaves. The s
says that children should be kept away from grass and trees. (AP WIRE
dsr11345bst amr/stf-boris yurchenko 1986

GRACE NICHOLS

Grace Nichols was born in 1950 in Guyana where she grew up and where, after university, she worked as a journalist and reporter. She moved to England in 1977 and has since developed her fiction and verse writing, publishing volumes for children and for adults.

Her poems show a strong sense of history – both her own and that of her Afro-Caribbean ancestry. Some poems offer warm memories of her Caribbean childhood ('Praise Song for My Mother'); others capture longer memories of slavery and oppression ('Taint'). Yet the oppression is not only of black people by white, but also of women by men. Her poems explore the role of the black woman living in a predominantly white society with irony and humour. Grace Nichols writes in both Standard English and Creole and often mixes the two, giving her poems sounds and rhythms that demand to be spoken aloud. Her use of Creole is another way of reclaiming her history and expressing her identity: while the words are English-based, the rhythm, intonation and structure of her language are influenced by West African speech patterns.

PRAISE SONG FOR MY MOTHER

You were
water to me
deep and bold and fathoming

You were
moon's eye to me
pull and grained and mantling

You were
sunrise to me
rise and warm and streaming

You were
the fishes red gill to me
the flame tree's spread to me
the crab's leg/the fried plantain smell
                          replenishing replenishing

Go to your wide futures, you said

WHEREVER I HANG

I leave me people, me land, me home
For reasons, I not too sure
I forsake de sun
And de humming-bird splendour
Had big rats in de floorboard
So I pick up me new-world-self
And come, to this place call England
At first I feeling like I in dream –
De misty greyness
I touching de walls to see if they real
They solid to de seam
And de people pouring from de underground system
Like beans
And when I look up to de sky
I see Lord Nelson high – too high to lie

And is so I sending home photos of myself
Among de pigeons and de snow
And is so I warding off de cold
And is so, little by little
I begin to change my calypso ways
Never visiting nobody
Before giving them clear warning
And waiting me turn in queue
Now, after all this time
I get accustom to de English life
But I still miss back-home side
To tell you de truth
I don't know really where I belaang

     Yes, divided to de ocean
     Divided to de bone

Wherever I hang me knickers – that's my home.

TAINT

But I was stolen by men
the colour of my own skin
borne away by men whose heels
had become hoofs
whose hands had turned talons
bearing me down
    to the trail
of darkness

But I was traded by men
the colour of my own skin
traded like a fowl   like a goat
like a sack of kernels I was
traded
    for beads   for pans
for trinkets?

No it isn't easy to forget
what we refuse to remember

Daily I rinse the taint
of treachery from my mouth

WE THE WOMEN

We the women who toil
unadorn
heads tie with cheap
cotton

We the women who cut
clear fetch dig sing

We the women making
something from this
ache-and-pain-a-me
back-o-hardness

Yet we the women
who praises go unsung
who voices go unheard
who deaths they sweep
aside
as easy as dead leaves

Tonight the fat black woman
is all agaze
will some Miss (plump at least
if not fat and black) uphold her name

The fat black woman awaits in vain
slim after slim aspirant appears
baring her treasures in hopeful despair
this the fat black woman can hardly bear

And as the beauties yearn
and the beauties yearn
the fat black woman wonders
when will the beauties
ever really burn

O the night wears on
the night wears on
judges mingling with chiffons

The fat black woman gets up
and pours some gin
toasting herself as a likely win

Of course when they ask for poems about the 'Realities' of black women

what they really want
at times
is a specimen
whose heart is in the dust

a mother-of-sufferer
trampled/oppressed
they want a little black blood
undressed
and validation
for the abused stereotype
already in their heads

       or else they want
       a perfect song

I say I can write
no poem big enough
to hold the essence

       of a black woman
       or a white woman
       or a green woman

and there are black women
and black women
              like a contrasting sky
of rainbow spectrum

touch a black woman
you mistake for a rock
and feel her melting
down to fudge

cradle a soft black woman
and burn fingers as you trace
revolution
beneath her woolly hair

and yes we cut bush
to clear paths
for our children
and yes we throw sprat
to catch whale
and yes
if need be we'll trade
a piece-a-pussy
that see the pickney dem
in the grip-a-hungry-belly

still there ain't no
easy belly category

       for a black woman
       or a white woman
       or a green woman

and there are black women
strong and eloquent
and focused

and there are black women
who somehow always manage to end up
frail victim

and there are black women
considered so dangerous
in South Africa
they prison them away

           maybe this poem is to say

that I like to see
we black women
full-of-we-selves walking

       crushing out
       with each dancing step
the twisted self-negating
history
we've inherited

       crushing out
       with each dancing step

JAMES BERRY

*J*ames Berry was born in a coastal village in Jamaica in 1924. He moved
to London in 1948 and has been living in Britain ever since. He
became a full-time writer in the late 1970s and published his first collection of
poems, *Lucy's Letters and Loving*, from which the first two poems printed here
are taken, in 1982. Since then, he has published several further volumes of
poems and a book of short stories drawing upon his childhood experiences in
Jamaica.

James Berry's poetry not only reflects both Jamaican and British language and
culture, but also merges them to create a variety of new voices for his
characters. His 'Lucy' poems are spoken by an uneducated immigrant woman,
the sister, as it were, of Grace Nichols' 'fat, black woman'. Whereas Lucy speaks
in Creole, Berry's young black English women ('Confession' and 'Young Woman
Reassesses') are portrayed in Standard English; in 'In-a Brixtan Markit', Tony is
given the language of streetwise black youth. All these poems show James
Berry's skill at capturing the experience of being black in Britain: the letters, the
reflections and the incidents all come alive when spoken aloud.

Things harness me here. I long
for we labrish* bad. Doors
not fixed open here.
No Leela either. No Cousin
Lil, Miss Lottie or Bro'-Uncle.
Dayclean doesn' have cockcrowin'.
Midmornin' doesn' bring
Cousin-Maa with her naseberry tray.
Afternoon doesn' give a ragged
Manwell, strung with fish
like bright leaves. Seven days
play same note in London, chile.
But Leela, money-rustle regular.

Me dear, I don' laugh now,
not'n' like we thunder claps
in darkness on verandah.
I turned a battery hen
in 'lectric light, day an' night.
No mood can touch one
mango season back at Yard.
At least though I did start
evening school once.
An' doctors free, chile.

London isn' like we
village dirt road, you know
Leela : it a parish
of a pasture-lan' what
grown crisscross streets,
an' they lie down to my door.
But I lock myself in.
I carry keys everywhere.
Life here's no open summer,
girl. But Sat'day mornin' don'
find me han' dry, don' find me face
a heavy cloud over the man.

* to gossip without restraint

An' though he still have
a weekend mind for bat'n'ball
he wash a dirty dish now, me dear.
It sweet him I on the Pill.
We get money for holidays
but there's no sun-hot
to enjoy cool breeze.

Leela, I really a sponge
you know, for traffic noise,
for work noise, for halfway
intentions, for halfway smiles,
for clockwatchin' an' col' weather.
I hope you don' think I gone
too fat when we meet.
I booked up to come an' soak
the children in daylight.

Yes, Leela, full teenagers now,
Tony an' Sharon. An' free at school
to work or squander time.
Thank God they hol' their own.
They body blemish free
an' you'd think they have no fear.

I did want them know the Bible,
know Shakespeare. Me dear, they
pity me. They say I still missing
links, I still don' understan'
world without black gods isn'
in worlds without end. The Buddha,
Mohammed, Jah, all
know the way they say.

They different breed, me dear.
The heads are Afro style.
They wear patches on the bum
to show they side with the poor.

Westindies is jus' a place parents
born: Bob Marley's their only thought
in it. 'Beat' sounds hypnotise them.
Beat-makers give them religion.

An' it's their joke I teachin'
me English neighbour Westindian Talk.
They eat'n' curry-an'-rice now
I say, they need little
Westindies Talk to season it.
They laugh at me an' say I funny.

Me dear, we all
lookin', lookin', lookin'.
Remember, 'One han' washes the other'.

I had a condition, she said.
I was born in England, you see.
Till last week, I was seventeen
years old. I've never seen
a Caribbean island, where my parents
came from. But I was born to know
black people had nothing. Black people
couldn't run their own countries,
couldn't take part in running the world.
Black people couldn't even run
a good two-people relationship.
They couldn't feed themselves, couldn't
make money, couldn't pass exams
and couldn't keep the law. And
black people couldn't get awards
on television. I asked my mother
why black people never achieved,
never explored, always got charity.
My mother said black people were cursed.
I knew.
I knew that.
I knew black people were cursed.
And I was one.
All the time I knew I was cursed.
Then going through a book on art
one night, a painting showed me
other people in struggle.
It showed me a different people like that.
Ragged, barefoot, hungry looking
they were in struggle.
I looked up.
The people needed: other people needed.
Or needed to remember their struggle.
Or even just to know
their need of struggle.
No. Not cursed.
Black people were not cursed.

I am told I enclose
the drives of a landscape
like a bunch of black grapes.

Just to stand at Oval Station
I get eyed like roast meat or get touched.
Any wonder I'm now a mask of stone?

I am told I conceal
warm rain and earth
in a fleshly fruit.

Hitchhiking I find friendly enemies
and have to take on
unknown highways.

Safe at last I go flying
with my talented and beautiful black boy.
I crash. I limp to the world for sympathy.

I am told, my eyes
and lips and all
unlock moments.

I release my international streak.
I go friendly.
My Rastaman all but kills me.

I bead my hair.
I tint my fingernails.
I colour my face.

I put on my best discoverable underwear
only to see my body is not
best friend to advise me.

I give myself to beauty contests.
I shine. I glitter. I bubble.
Hot baths become best friend.

Any wonder I want
a new style
for country and for town?

Absorbed deeply in a landscape I learn
I have a mistaken voice
calling for company.

IN-A BRIXTAN MARKIT

I walk in-a Brixtan markit,
believin I a respectable man,
you know. An wha happn?

Policeman come straight up
an search mi bag!
Man – straight to mi.
Like them did a-wait fi mi.
Come search mi bag, man.

Fi mi bag!
An wha them si in deh?
Two piece a yam, a dasheen,
a han a banana, a piece a pork
an mi lates Bob Marley.

Man all a suddn I feel
mi head nah fi mi. This yah now
is when man kill somody, nah!

'Tony', I sey, 'hol on. Hol on,
Tony. Dohn shove. Dohn shove.
Dohn move neidda fis, tongue
nor emotion. Battn down, Tony.
Battn down.' An, man, Tony win.

Still a shock to remember, facing
that attacking dog's fangs and eyes
at its gate;
seeing our slug-eating dog come in
the house, mouth gummed up, plastered!

Still a joy to remember, standing
at our palm-fringed beach
watching sunrise streak the sea;
finding a hen's nest in high grass
full of eggs;
riding a horse bareback, galloping.

Still a shock to remember, eating
with fingers and caught oily-handed
by my teacher;
seeing a dog like goat-hide flattened
there in the road.

Still a joy to remember, myself
a small boy milking a cow
in new sunlight;
smelling asafoetida
on a village baby I held;
sucking fresh honey from its comb
just robbed.

Still a shock to remember, watching
weighted kittens tossed in the sea's
white breakers;
seeing our village stream dried up
with rocks exposed
like dry guts and brains.

Still a joy to remember, walking
barefoot on a bed of dry leaves
there in deep woods;
finding my goat with all of three
new wobbly kids.

Still a shock to remember, facing
that youth-gang attack and all
the needless abuse;
holding my first identity card
stamped 'Negro'.

Still a joy to remember, walking
fourteen miles from four a.m.
into town market;
surrounded by sounds of church-bell
in sunlight and birdsong.

TED HUGHES

A Yorkshireman whose father was a carpenter, Ted Hughes was born in 1930 at Mytholmroyd. When he was seven, the family moved to the mining town of Mexborough where his parents ran a newsagent's and tobacconist's shop. After completing his National Service, he went to Cambridge and subsequently worked in a number of jobs before becoming a teacher. His first wife was the American poet Sylvia Plath.

Since his first book, *The Hawk in the Rain* (1957), he has published many volumes of poetry, both for children and for the general reader. Since 1984, Ted Hughes has been Poet Laureate.

His poems are often dark and violent, and images of physical power frequently recur. His world of nature is harsh and bleak – even the snowdrop is metallic and brutal: the slow grinding of the evolutionary process and the battle for survival dominate. The arch-survivor, man, is seen in the form of Crow – the incorrigible and amoral creation who knows how to bend the rules.

In a talk which Ted Hughes recorded for the BBC a few years ago, he began by recalling his childhood love of animals. As a boy, living first in a Pennine Valley in West Yorkshire and later in an industrial town in South Yorkshire, he spent a good deal of time hunting and trapping, retrieving birds and animals which his brother shot, fishing in the local canal, and drawing and modelling creatures for his own pictorial zoo. He went on:

. . . at about fifteen my life grew more complicated and my attitude to animals changed. I accused myself of disturbing their lives. I began to look at them, you see, from their own point of view.

And about the same time I began to write poems. Not animal poems. It was years before I wrote what you could call an animal poem and several more years before it occurred to me that my writing poems might be partly a continuation of my earlier pursuit. Now I have no doubt. The special kind of excitement, the slightly mesmerised and quite involuntary concentration with which you make out the stirrings of a new poem in your mind, then the outline, the mass and colour and clean final form of it, the unique living reality of it in the midst of the general lifelessness, all that is too familiar to mistake. This is hunting and the poem is a new species of creature, a new specimen of the life outside your own . . .

Some of [this] may seem a bit obscure to you. How can a poem, for instance, about a walk in the rain, be like an animal? Well, perhaps it cannot look much like a giraffe or an emu or an octopus, or anything you might find in a menagerie. It is better to call it an assembly of living parts moved by a single spirit. The living parts are the words, the images, the rhythms. The spirit is the life which inhabits them when they all work together. It is impossible to say which comes first, parts or spirit. But if any of the parts are dead . . . if any of the words, or images or rhythms do not jump to life as you read them . . . then the creature is going to be maimed and the spirit sickly. So, as a poet, you have to make sure that all those parts over which you have control, the words and rhythms and images, are alive. That is where the difficulties begin. Yet the rules to begin with are very simple. Words which live are those which we hear, like 'click' or 'chuckle', or which we see, like 'freckled' or 'veined', or which we taste, like 'vinegar' or 'sugar', or touch, like 'prickle' or 'oily', or smell, like 'tar' or 'onion'. Words which belong directly to one of the five senses. Or words which act and seem to use their muscles, like 'flick' or 'balance'.

But immediately things become more difficult. 'Click' not only gives you a sound, it gives you the notion of a sharp movement . . . such as your tongue makes in saying 'click'. It also gives you the feel of something light and brittle – like a snapping twig. Heavy things do not click, nor do soft bendable ones. In the same way, tar not only smells strongly. It is sticky to touch, with a particular thick and choking stickiness. Also it moves, when it is soft, like a black snake, and has a beautiful black gloss. So it is with most words. They belong to several of the senses at once, as if each one had eyes, ears and tongue, or ears and fingers and a body to move with. It is this little goblin in a word which is its life and its poetry, and it is this goblin which the poet has to have under control.

Well, you will say, this is hopeless. How do you control all that. When the words are pouring out, how can you be sure that you do not have one of these side meanings of the word 'feathers' stuck up with one of the side meanings of the word 'treacle', a few words later. In bad poetry this is exactly what happens, the words kill each other. Luckily, you do not have to bother about it so long as you do one thing.

That one thing is to imagine what you are writing about. See it and live it. Do not think it up laboriously, as if you were working out mental arithmetic. Just look at it, touch it, smell it, listen to it, turn yourself into it. When you do this, the words look after themselves like magic. If you do this you do not have to bother about commas or full-stops or that sort of thing. You do not look at the words either. You keep your eyes, your ears, your nose, your taste, your touch, your whole being on the thing you are turning into words. The minute you flinch, and take your mind off this thing, and begin to look at the words and worry about them . . . then your worry goes into them and they set about killing each other. So you keep going as long as you can, then look back and see what you have written. After a bit of practice, and after telling yourself a few times that you do not care how other people have written about this thing, this is the way you find it; and after telling yourself that you are going to use any old word that comes into your head so long as it seems right at the moment of writing it down, you will surprise yourself. You will read back through what you have written and you will get a shock. You will have captured a spirit, a creature . . .

An animal I never succeeded in keeping alive is the fox. I was always
frustrated: twice by a farmer, who killed cubs I had caught before I could get to
them, and once by a poultry keeper who freed my cub while his dog waited.
Years after those events I was sitting up late one snowy night in dreary lodgings
in London. I had written nothing for a year or so but that night I got the idea
I might write something and I wrote in a few minutes the following poem: the
first 'animal' poem I ever wrote. Here it is:

THE THOUGHT-FOX

I imagine this midnight moment's forest:
Something else is alive
Beside the clock's loneliness
And this blank page where my fingers move.

Through the window I see no star:
Something more near
Though deeper within darkness
Is entering the loneliness:

Cold, delicately as the dark snow,
A fox's nose touches twig, leaf;
Two eyes serve a movement, that now
And again now, and now, and now

Sets neat prints into the snow
Between trees, and warily a lame
Shadow lags by stump and in hollow
Of a body that is bold to come

Across clearings, an eye,
A widening deepening greenness,
Brilliantly, concentratedly,
Coming about its own business

Till, with a sudden sharp hot stink of fox
It enters the dark hole of the head.
The window is starless still; the clock ticks,
The page is printed.

This poem does not have anything you could easily call a meaning. It is about
a fox, obviously enough, but a fox that is both a fox and not a fox. What sort
of fox is it that can step right into my head where presumably it still sits . . .
smiling to itself when the dogs bark. It is both a fox and a spirit. It is a real
fox; as I read the poem I see it move, I see it setting its prints, I see its shadow
going over the irregular surface of the snow. The words show me all this,
bringing it nearer and nearer. It is very real to me. The words have made a
body for it and given it somewhere to walk.

(From *Capturing Animals* by Ted Hughes)

1

The sun lies mild and still on the yard stones.

The clue is a solitary daffodil – the first.

And the whole air struggling in soft excitements
Like a woman hurrying into her silks.
Birds everywhere zipping and unzipping
Changing their minds, in soft excitements,
Warming their wings and trying their voices.

The trees still spindle bare.

Beyond them, from the warmed blue hills
An exhilaration swirls upward, like a huge fish.

As under a waterfall, in the bustling pool.

Over the whole land
Spring thunders down in brilliant silence.

5
Spring bulges the hills.
The bare trees creak and shift.
Some buds have burst in tatters –
Like firework stubs.

But winter's lean bullocks
Only pretend to eat
The grass that will not come.

Then they bound like lambs, they twist in the air
They bounce their half tons of elastic
When the bale of hay breaks open.

They gambol from heap to heap,
Finally stand happy chewing their beards
Of last summer's dusty whiskers.

6

With arms swinging, a tremendous skater
On the flimsy ice of space,
The earth leans into its curve –

Thrilled to the core, some flies have waded out
An inch onto my window, to stand on the sky
And try their buzz.

SNOWDROP

Now is the globe shrunk tight
Round the mouse's dulled wintering heart.
Weasel and crow, as if moulded in brass,
Move through an outer darkness
Not in their right minds,
With the other deaths. She, too, pursues her ends,
Brutal as the stars of this month,
Her pale head heavy as metal.

TELEGRAPH WIRES

Take telegraph wires, a lonely moor,
And fit them together. The thing comes alive in your ear.

Towns whisper to towns over the heather.
But the wires cannot hide from the weather.

So oddly, so daintily made
It is picked up and played.

Such unearthly airs
The ear hears, and withers!

In the revolving ballroom of space,
Bowed over the moor, a bright face

Draws out of telegraph wires the tones
That empty human bones.

Who owns these scrawny little feet? *Death.*
Who owns this bristly scorched-looking face? *Death.*
Who owns these still-working lungs? *Death.*
Who owns this utility coat of muscles? *Death.*
Who owns these unspeakable guts? *Death.*
Who owns these questionable brains? *Death.*
All this messy blood? *Death.*
These minimum-efficiency eyes? *Death.*
This wicked little tongue? *Death.*
This occasional wakefulness? *Death.*

Given, stolen, or held pending trial? *Held.*

Who owns the whole rainy, stony earth? *Death.*
Who owns all of space? *Death.*

Who is stronger than hope? *Death.*
Who is stronger than the will? *Death.*
Stronger than love? *Death.*
Stronger than life? *Death.*

But who is stronger than death?
Me, evidently.

CROW'S SONG OF HIMSELF

When God hammered Crow
He made gold
When God roasted Crow in the sun
He made diamond
When God crushed Crow under weights
He made alcohol
When God tore Crow to pieces
He made money
When God blew Crow up
He made day
When God hung Crow on a tree
He made fruit
When God buried Crow in the earth
He made man
When God tried to chop Crow in two
He made woman
When God said: 'You win, Crow,'
He made the Redeemer.

When God went off in despair
Crow stropped his beak and started in on the two thieves.

KING OF CARRION

His palace is of skulls.

His crown is the last splinters
Of the vessel of life.

His throne is the scaffold of bones, the hanged thing's
Rack and final stretcher.

His robe is the black of the last blood.

His kingdom is empty –

The empty world, from which the last cry
Flapped hugely, hopelessly away
Into the blindness and dumbness and deafness of the gulf

Returning, shrunk, silent

To reign over silence.

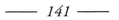

SEAMUS HEANEY

In 1972 Seamus Heaney left Belfast's Queens University to live in County Wicklow in the Republic of Ireland, and to devote himself full time to writing. For three years he made his living as a freelance writer, returning to Dublin in 1976. In 1984 he was appointed to a professorship at Harvard, and in 1989 he became Professor of Poetry at Oxford, two posts which have taken him away from Ireland for long periods, but which have also given him time to pursue his own work.

In an article reflecting on his own development as a poet, Seamus Heaney suggests a link between what he regards as his first successful poem, 'Digging', and his later 'bog poems', such as 'The Grauballe Man' and 'Punishment'.

In the following four extracts, Heaney writes about 'feeling into words' (the title of his article) and describes how the symbolism of the peat bog, present from the start, gathered significance as his writing developed.

*S*eamus Heaney writes:

Possibly the most relevant fact is the removal from a rural to an urban environment – death of a naturalist, partly. I was born in 1939 on a farm in County Derry and I grew up in a community where traditional methods of farming – horse-ploughs, mowing with scythes, hand-threshing – were still in operation. My father was also a cattle-dealer and I saw much of the cattle-fairs of the Ulster countryside.

His appointment as a university lecturer and the passage of time meant change.

. . . [the] death of a traditional way of life, and the sense of loss which I experienced in my new academic environment are probably the most pertinent feelings. I am the eldest son of a family of eight children, three of whom still work on the farm.

'Digging': the pen as spade

'Digging', in fact, was the name of the first poem I wrote where I thought my feelings had got into words, or to put it more accurately, where I thought my feel had got into words. Its rhythms and noises still please me, although there are a couple of lines in it that have more of the theatricality of the gunslinger than the self-absorption of the digger. I wrote it in the summer of 1964, almost two years after I had begun to 'dabble in verses'. This was the first place where I felt that I had done more than make an arrangement of words: I felt that I had let down a shaft into real life. The facts and surfaces of the thing were true, but more important, the excitement that came from naming them gave me a kind of insouciance and a kind of confidence. I didn't care who thought what about it: somehow, it had surprised me by coming out with a stance and an idea that I would stand over:

> The cold smell of potato mould, the squelch and slap
> Of soggy peat, the curt cuts of an edge
> Through living roots awaken in my head.
> But I've no spade to follow men like them.
>
> Between my finger and my thumb
> The squat pen rests.
> I'll dig with it.

As I say, I wrote it down years ago; yet perhaps I should say that I dug it up, because I have come to realise that it was laid down in me years before that even. The pen/spade analogy was the simple heart of the matter and that was simply a matter of almost proverbial common sense. As a child on the road to and from school, people used to ask you what class you were in and how many slaps you'd got that day and invariably they ended up with an exhortation to keep studying because 'learning's easy carried' and 'the pen's lighter than the spade'. And the poem does no more than allow that bud of wisdom to exfoliate, although the significant point in this context is that at the time of writing I was not aware of the proverbial structure at the back of my mind.

Finding a voice

I was getting my first sense of crafting words and for one reason or another, words as bearers of history and mystery began to invite me. Maybe it began very early when my mother used to recite lists of affixes and suffixes, and Latin roots, with their English meanings, rhymes that formed part of her schooling in the early part of the century. Maybe it began with the exotic listing on the wireless dial: Stuttgart, Leipzig, Oslo, Hilversum. Maybe it was stirred by the beautiful sprung rhythms of the old BBC weather forecast: Dogger, Rockall, Malin, Shetland, Faroes, Finisterre; or with the gorgeous and inane phraseology of the catechism; or with the litany of the Blessed Virgin that was part of the enforced poetry in our household: Tower of Gold, Ark of the Covenant, Gate of Heaven, Morning Star, Health of the Sick, Refuge of Sinners, Comforter of the Afflicted. None of these things were consciously savoured at the time but I think the fact that I still recall them with ease, and can delight in them as verbal music, means that they were bedding the ear with a kind of linguistic hardcore that could be built on some day.

That was the unconscious bedding, but poetry involves a conscious savouring of words also. This came by way of reading poetry itself, and being required to learn pieces by heart, phrases even, like Keats's, from 'Lamia':

> and his vessel now
> Grated the quaystone with her brazen prow,

or Wordsworth's:

> All shod with steel,
> We hiss'd along the polished ice,

or Tennyson's:

> Old yew, which graspest at the stones
> That name the underlying dead,
> Thy fibres net the dreamless head,
> Thy roots are wrapped about the bones.

These were picked up in my last years at school, touchstones of sorts, where the language could give you a kind of aural gooseflesh.

'Bogland': the landscape of memory

I had been vaguely wishing to write a poem about bogland, chiefly because it is a landscape that has a strange assuaging effect on me, one with associations reaching back into early childhood. We used to hear about bog-butter, butter kept fresh for a great number of years under the peat. Then when I was at school the skeleton of an elk had been taken out of a bog nearby and a few of our neighbours had got their photographs in the paper, peering out across its antlers. So I began to get an idea of bog as the memory of the landscape, or as a landscape that remembered everything that happened in and to it. In fact, if you go round the National Museum in Dublin, you will realise that a great proportion of the most cherished material heritage of Ireland was 'found in a bog'. Moreover, since memory was the faculty that supplied me with the first quickening of my own poetry, I had a tentative unrealised need to make a congruence between memory and bogland and, for the want of a better word, our national consciousness. And it all released itself after 'We have no prairies . . .' – but we have bogs.

At that time I was teaching modern literature in Queen's University, Belfast, and had been reading about the frontier and the west as an important myth in the American consciousness, so I set up – or rather, laid down – the bog as an answering Irish myth. I wrote it quickly the next morning, having slept on my excitement, and revised it on the hoof, from line to line, as it came:

BOGLAND

We have no prairies
To slice a big sun at evening –
Everywhere the eye concedes to
Encroaching horizon,

Is wooed into the cyclops' eye
Of a tarn. Our unfenced country
Is bog that keeps crusting
Between the sights of the sun.

They've taken the skeleton
Of the great Irish Elk
Out of the peat, set it up
An astounding crate full of air.

Butter sunk under
More than a hundred years
Was recovered salty and white.
The ground itself is kind, black butter

Melting and opening underfoot,
Missing its last definition
By millions of years.
They'll never dig coal here,

Only the waterlogged trunks
Of great firs, soft as pulp.
Our pioneers keep striking
Inwards and downwards,

Every layer they strip
Seems camped on before.
The bogholes might be Atlantic seepage.
The wet centre is bottomless.

Again, as in the case of 'Digging', the seminal impulse had been unconscious. What generated the poem about memory was something lying beneath the very floor of memory, something I only connected with the poem months after it was written, which was a warning that older people would give us about going into the bog. They were afraid we might fall into the pools in the old workings so they put it about (and we believed them) that there was no bottom *in the bog-holes.*

Two 'Bog Poems': 'The Grauballe Man' and 'Punishment'

With the eruption of the 'troubles' in Ireland in August 1969, Heaney diagnosed the Irish poet's task as 'a search for images and symbols adequate to our predicament', a search for 'befitting emblems of adversity'. He continues:

> *Some of these emblems I found in a book that was published in English translation, appositely, the year the killing started, in 1969. And again appositely, it was entitled* The Bog People. *It was chiefly concerned with preserved bodies of men and women found in the bogs of Jutland, naked, strangled or with their throats cut, disposed under the peat since early Iron Age times. The author, P. V. Glob, argues convincingly that a number of these, and in particular the Tollund Man, whose head is now preserved near Aarhus in the museum at Silkeburg, were ritual sacrifices to the Mother Goddess, the goddess of the ground who needed new bridegrooms each winter to bed with her in her sacred place, in the bog, to ensure the renewal and fertility of the territory in the spring. Taken in relation to the tradition of Irish political martyrdom for that cause whose icon is Kathleen Ni Houlihan, this is more than an archaic barbarous rite: it is an archetypal pattern. And the unforgettable photographs of these victims blended in my mind with photographs of atrocities, past and present, in the long rites of Irish political and religious struggles.*

(Extracts from 'Feeling into Words' in *Selected Prose* by Seamus Heaney)

DIGGING

Between my finger and my thumb
The squat pen rests; snug as a gun.

Under my window, a clean rasping sound
When the spade sinks into gravelly ground:
My father, digging. I look down

Till his straining rump among the flowerbeds
Bends low, comes up twenty years away
Stooping in rhythm through potato drills
Where he was digging.

The coarse boot nestled on the lug, the shaft
Against the inside knee was levered firmly.
He rooted out tall tops, buried the bright edge deep
To scatter new potatoes that we picked
Loving their cool hardness in our hands.

By God, the old man could handle a spade.
Just like his old man.

My grandfather cut more turf in a day
Than any other man on Toner's bog.
Once I carried him milk in a bottle
Corked sloppily with paper. He straightened up
To drink it, then fell to right away

Nicking and slicing neatly, heaving sods
Over his shoulder, going down and down
For the good turf. Digging.

The cold smell of potato mould, the squelch and slap
Of soggy peat, the curt cuts of an edge
Through living roots awaken in my head.
But I've no spade to follow men like them.

Between my finger and my thumb
The squat pen rests.
I'll dig with it.

PERSONAL HELICON*

For Michael Longley

As a child, they could not keep me from wells
And old pumps with buckets and windlasses.
I loved the dark drop, the trapped sky, the smells
Of waterweed, fungus and dank moss.

One, in a brickyard, with a rotted board top.
I savoured the rich crash when a bucket
Plummeted down at the end of a rope.
So deep you saw no reflection in it.

A shallow one under a dry stone ditch
Fructified like any aquarium.
When you dragged out long roots from the soft mulch
A white face hovered over the bottom.

Others had echoes, gave back your own call
With a clean new music in it. And one
Was scaresome for there, out of ferns and tall
Foxgloves, a rat slapped across my reflection.

Now, to pry into roots, to finger slime,
To stare big-eyed Narcissus, into some spring
Is beneath all adult dignity. I rhyme
To see myself, to set the darkness echoing.

*a mountain in Greece, sacred to the Muses, one of which was poetry

The tightness and the nilness round that space
when the car stops in the road, the troops inspect
its make and number and, as one bends his face

towards your window, you catch sight of more
on a hill beyond, eyeing with intent
down cradled guns that hold you under cover

and everything is pure interrogation
until a rifle motions and you move
with guarded unconcerned acceleration –

a little emptier, a little spent
as always by that quiver in the self,
subjugated, yes, and obedient.

So you drive on to the frontier of writing
where it happens again. The guns on tripods;
the sergeant with his on-off mike repeating

data about you, waiting for the squawk
of clearance; the marksman training down
out of the sun upon you like a hawk.

And suddenly you're through, arraigned yet freed,
as if you'd passed from behind a waterfall
on the black current of a tarmac road

past armour-plated vehicles, out between
the posted soldiers flowing and receding
like tree shadows into the polished windscreen.

For Philip Hobsbaum

Late August, given heavy rain and sun
For a full week, the blackberries would ripen.
At first, just one, a glossy purple clot
Among others, red, green, hard as a knot.
You ate that first one and its flesh was sweet
Like thickened wine: summer's blood was in it
Leaving stains upon the tongue and lust for
Picking. Then red ones inked up and that hunger
Sent us out with milk-cans, pea-tins, jam-pots
Where briars scratched and wet grass bleached our boots.
Round hayfields, cornfields and potato-drills
We trekked and picked until the cans were full,
Until the tinkling bottom had been covered
With green ones, and on top big dark blobs burned
Like a plate of eyes. Our hands were peppered
With thorn pricks, our palms sticky as Bluebeard's.

We hoarded the fresh berries in the byre.
But when the bath was filled we found a fur,
A rat-grey fungus, glutting on our cache.
The juice was stinking too. Once off the bush
The fruit fermented, the sweet flesh would turn sour.
I always felt like crying. It wasn't fair
That all the lovely canfuls smelt of rot.
Each year I hoped they'd keep, knew they would not.

LIMBO

Fishermen at Ballyshannon
Netted an infant last night
Along with the salmon.
An illegitimate spawning,

A small one thrown back
To the waters. But I'm sure
As she stood in the shallows
Ducking him tenderly

Till the frozen knobs of her wrists
Were as dead as the gravel,
He was a minnow with hooks
Tearing her open.

She waded in under
The sign of her cross.
He was hauled in with the fish.
Now limbo will be

A cold glitter of souls
Through some far briny zone.
Even Christ's palms, unhealed,
Smart and cannot fish there.

As if he had been poured
in tar, he lies
on a pillow of turf
and seems to weep

the black river of himself.
The grain of his wrists
is like bog oak,
the ball of his heel

like a basalt egg.
His instep has shrunk
cold as a swan's foot
or a wet swamp root.

His hips are the ridge
and purse of a mussel,
his spine an eel arrested
under a glisten of mud.

The head lifts,
the chin is a visor
raised above the vent
of his slashed throat

that has tanned and toughened.
The cured wound
opens inwards to a dark
elderberry place.

Who will say 'corpse'
to his vivid cast?
Who will say 'body'
to his opaque repose?

And his rusted hair,
a mat unlikely
as a foetus's.
I first saw his twisted face

in a photograph,
a head and shoulder
out of the peat,
bruised like a forceps baby,

but now he lies
perfected in my memory,
down to the red horn
of his nails,

hung in the scales
with beauty and atrocity:
with the Dying Gaul
too strictly compassed

on his shield,
with the actual weight
of each hooded victim,
slashed and dumped.

I can feel the tug
of the halter at the nape
of her neck, the wind
on her naked front.

It blows her nipples
to amber beads,
it shakes the frail rigging
of her ribs.

I can see her drowned
body in the bog,
the weighing stone,
the floating rods and boughs.

Under which at first
she was a barked sapling
that is dug up
oak-bone, brain-firkin:

her shaved head
like a stubble of black corn,
her blindfold a soiled bandage,
her noose a ring

to store
the memories of love.
Little adulteress,
before they punished you

you were flaxen-haired,
undernourished, and your
tar-black face was beautiful.
My poor scapegoat,

I almost love you
but would have cast, I know,
the stones of silence.
I am the artful voyeur

of your brain's exposed
and darkened combs,
your muscles' webbing
and all your numbered bones:

I who have stood dumb
when your betraying sisters,
cauled in tar,
wept by the railings,

who would connive
in civilized outrage
yet understand the exact
and tribal, intimate revenge.

ROGER MCGOUGH

*R*oger McGough's poems gained wide publicity in the late 1960s when he was a member of the group known as 'The Liverpool Poets' who wrote and performed their verses in the aftermath of the success of The Beatles. He was born in Liverpool in 1937 and for a time was a member of the pop group The Scaffold. With the other Liverpool poets – Brian Patten and Adrian Henri – he has published *The Mersey Sound* (1967) and *New Volume* (1983), as well as producing several books of his own verse.

His style is usually light and colloquial; he enjoys puns and wordplay. There is a freshness and humour about his writing which comes over best when his poems are read aloud. Yet, as several of these poems show, his informal voice can also speak thoughtfully about larger themes ('Three Rusty Nails'), about family relationships ('The Railings' and 'Just Passing'), and about sensitive social problems ('Who are These Men?').

Do people who wave at trains
Wave at the driver, or at the train itself?
Or, do people who wave at trains
Wave at the passengers? Those hurtling strangers,
The unidentifiable flying faces?

They must think we like being waved at.
Children do perhaps, and alone
In a compartment, the occasional passenger
Who is himself a secret waver at trains.
But most of us are unimpressed.

Some even think they're daft.
Stuck out there in a field, grinning.
But our ignoring them, our blank faces,
Even our pulled tongues and up you signs
Come three miles further down the line.

Out of harm's way by then
They continue their walk.
Refreshed and made pure, by the mistaken belief
That their love has been returned,
Because they have not seen it rejected.

It's like God in a way. Another day
Another universe. Always off somewhere.
And left behind, the faithful few,
Stuck out there. Not a care in the world.
All innocence. Arms in the air. Waving.

A baby rabbit fell into a quarry's mixing machine yesterday and came out in the middle of a concrete block. But the rabbit still had the strength to dig its way free before the block set.

The tiny creature was scooped up with 30 tons of sand, then swirled and pounded through the complete mixing process. Mr Michael Hooper, the machine operator, found the rabbit shivering on top of the solid concrete block, its coat stiff with fragments. A hole from the middle of the block and paw marks showed the escape route.

Mr Reginald Denslow, manager of J. R. Pratt and Sons' quarry at Kilmington, near Axminster, Devon, said: 'This rabbit must have a lot more than nine lives to go through this machine. I just don't know how it avoided being suffocated, ground, squashed or cut in half.' With the 30 tons of sand, it was dropped into a weighing hopper and carried by conveyor to an overhead mixer where it was whirled around with gallons of water.

From there the rabbit was swept to a machine which hammers wet concrete into blocks by pressure of 100 lb per square inch. The rabbit was encased in a block eighteen inches long, nine inches high and six inches thick. Finally the blocks were ejected on to the floor to dry and the dazed rabbit clawed itself free. 'We cleaned him up, dried him by the electric fire, then he hopped away,' Mr Denslow said.

Daily Telegraph

'Tell us a story Grandad'
The bunny rabbits implored
'About the block of concrete
Out of which you clawed.'

'Tell every gory detail
Of how you struggled free
From the teeth of the Iron Monster
And swam through a quicksand sea.'

'How you battled with the Humans
(And the part we like the most)
Your escape from the raging fire
When they held you there to roast.'

The old adventurer smiled
And waved a wrinkled paw
'All right children, settle down
I'll tell it just once more.'

His thin nose started twitching
Near-blind eyes began to flood
As the part that doesn't age
Drifted back to bunnyhood.

When spring was king of the seasons
And days were built to last
When thunder was merely thunder
Not a distant quarry blast.

How, leaving the warren one morning
Looking for somewhere to play
He'd wandered far into the woods
And there had lost his way.

When suddenly without warning
The earth gave way, and he fell
Off the very edge of the world
Into the darkness of Hell.

Sharp as the colour of a carrot
On a new-born bunny's tongue
Was the picture he recalled
Of that day when he was young.

Trance-formed now by the memory
His voice was close to tears
But the story he was telling
Was falling on deaf ears.

There was giggling and nudging
And lots of 'Sssh – he'll hear'
For it was a trick, a game they played
Grown crueller with each year.

'Poor old Grandad' they tittered
As they one by one withdrew
'He's told it all so often
He now believes it's true.'

Young rabbits need fresh carrots
And his had long grown stale
So they left the old campaigner
Imprisoned in his tale.

Petrified by memories
Haunting ever strong
Encased in a block of time
Eighteen inches long.

*　*　*

Alone in a field in Devon
An old rabbit is sitting, talking,
When out of the wood, at the edge of the
world,
A man with a gun comes walking.

THE RAILINGS

You came to watch me playing cricket once.
Quite a few of the fathers did.
At ease, outside the pavilion
they would while away a Saturday afternoon.
Joke with the masters, urge on
their flannelled offspring. But not you.

Fielding deep near the boundary
I saw you through the railings.
You were embarrassed when I waved
and moved out of sight down the road.
When it was my turn to bowl though
I knew you'd still be watching.

Third ball, a wicket, and three more followed.
When we came in at the end of the innings
the other dads applauded and joined us for tea.
Of course, you had gone by then. Later,
you said you'd found yourself there by accident.
Just passing. Spotted me through the railings.

*   *   *

Speech-days . Prize-givings . School-plays
The Twentyfirst . The Wedding . The Christening
You would find yourself there by accident.
Just passing. Spotted me through the railings.

JUST PASSING

Just passing, I spot you through the railings.
You don't see me. Why should you?
Outside the gates, I am out of your orbit.

Break-time for Infants and first-year Juniors
and the playground is a microcosmos:
planets, asteroids, molecules, chromosomes.

Constellations swirling, a genetic whirlpool
Worlds within worlds. A Russian doll
of universes bursting at each seam.

Here and there, some semblance of order
as those who would benefit from rules
are already seeking to impose them.

Not yet having to make sense of it all
you are in tune with chaos, at its centre.
Third son lucky, at play, oblivious of railings.

I try and catch your eye. To no avail.
Wave goodbye anyway, and pocketing
my notebook, move on. Someday we must talk.

Mother, there's a strange man
Waiting at the door
With a familiar sort of face
You feel you've seen before.

Says his name is Jesus
Can we spare a couple of bob
Says he's been made redundant
And now can't find a job.

Yes I think he is a foreigner
Egyptian or a Jew
Oh aye, and that reminds me
He'd like some water too.

Well shall I give him what he wants
Or send him on his way?
OK I'll give him 5p
Say that's all we've got today.

And I'll forget about the water
I suppose it's a bit unfair
But honest, he's filthy dirty
All beard and straggly hair.

*   *   *

Mother, he asked about the water
I said the tank had burst
Anyway I gave him the coppers
That seemed to quench his thirst.

He said it was little things like that
That kept him on the rails
Then he gave me his autographed picture
And these three rusty nails.

Who are these men who would do you harm?
Not the mad-eyed who grumble at pavements
Banged up in a cell with childhood ghosts

Who shout suddenly and frighten you. Not they.
The men who would do you harm have gentle voices
Have practised their smiles in front of mirrors.

Disturbed as children, they are disturbed by them.
Obsessed. They wear kindness like a carapace
Day-dreaming up ways of cajoling you into the car.

Unattended, they are devices impatient
To explode. Ignore the helping hand
It will clench. Beware the lap, it is a trapdoor.

They are the spies in our midst. In the park,
Outside the playground, they watch and wait.
Given half a chance, love, they would take you

Undo you. Break you into a million pieces.
Perhaps, in time, I would learn forgiveness.
Perhaps, in time, I would kill one.

Workshop

Group presentation (eight groups, one on each poet)

The aim is to get to know the poems of each writer.

Each group prepares a presentation for the rest of the class on one of the poets in this section. Your presentation should last about ten minutes and include:

- some introductory comments, relevant background details, and, perhaps, one or two quotations from the poems that best represent the poet's work;

- linked readings of the other poems. You will need to decide the order of the poems and whose voices you are going to use. Prepare some brief connecting comments to link the readings;

- a summary of, say, three or four main points that you notice about the writer.

Individual work on a poet or a topic

The aim is to compile a folder of coursework to include the following:

- a cover design which captures the main themes of your chosen poet or topic;

- a contents list of items in your folder;

- a collection of favourite lines and phrases, with a note to say what you like about each;

- an open letter to one or more of the poets, saying which poems you like and why, and raising any questions you might have. (These can be followed up in class discussion);

- your favourite poem with your own responses to it 'mapped' in note form around the text. You will need to copy out the poem carefully in the centre of a page and then, with a pen of a different colour, make your notes. Underneath, complete the single sentence: 'I like this poem because . . .';

- a pastiche poem of your own; that is, one written in the same style as one of these poets;

- *on the poet*: an essay describing what you think are the main qualities of your chosen poet. Comment on the subjects the writer deals with and the language, forms, feelings and ideas that you notice in the poems you discuss;

- *on the topic*: an essay about the main aspects of the topic you have chosen and the ways that different poets write about it. Include your ideas about the writers' attitudes to the topic. How are these attitudes reflected in the words they use and the tones of voice they adopt?

Whether you choose to write about a poet or a topic, the following notes and references are designed to help you. You will need to discuss the scope of your work with your teacher and to follow up some of the references in the library.

POETS

There is plenty of variety in the eight poets represented here. (If, in discussion with your teacher, you opt to work on another poet instead, be sure that there is enough 'substance' in your choice – that you have access to enough poems and that you have enough to say about them.)

Sylvia Plath   See also 'The Arrival of the Bee Box' (p. 15), 'Morning Song' (p. 23) and 'Metaphors' (p. 22). *Collected Poems*, Faber and Faber.

U. A. Fanthorpe   *Selected Poems*, Penguin; *Neck Verse*, Peterloo Press.

Gillian Clarke   *Selected Poems*, Carcanet; *Letting in the Rumour*, Carcanet.

Grace Nichols   *The Fat Black Woman's Poems*, Virago.

James Berry   *Chain of Days*, Oxford University Press.

Ted Hughes   *Season Songs*, Faber and Faber; *New Selected Poems, 1957–94*, Faber and Faber.

Seamus Heaney   See also 'The Early Purges' (p. 5); *New Selected Poems, 1966–87*, Faber and Faber.

Roger McGough   See also 'The Hippopotamusman' (p. 72) and 'Watchwords' (p. 80). *Blazing Fruit. Selected Poems 1967–87*, Penguin; *Defying Gravity*, Penguin.

TOPICS

Either take up one of the four topics outlined below or, in discussion with your teacher, devise your own.

1   Caribbean and Black British Poetry

Start with the work of James Berry and Grace Nichols, but also look at John Agard's poems (pp. 73 and 74) and his collection *Mangoes and Bullets* (Pluto Press). You might like to look at some general anthologies, including *News for Babylon*, edited by James Berry (Chatto and Windus) and *Hinterland*, edited by E. A. Markham (Bloodaxe).

What appeals to you in the poems of black writers?

2 Poetry by Women

Start with the work of the four women poets presented here, but also look at the poems of other writers in *Poetry Workshop*, for example May Swenson, Stevie Smith, Denise Levertov, Emily Dickinson, Elaine Feinstein, Carol Ann Duffy and Liz Lochhead. Several collections of women's poetry are now available, including *Six Women Poets*, edited by Judith Kinsman (Oxford Student Texts) and *Sixty Women Poets*, edited by Linda France (Bloodaxe).

Is there any evidence that women write about different things and in different ways from men?

3 People and Relationships

Browse through the poems by these eight writers and list, say, six poems that appeal to you which portray particular characters, or which capture the relationships between people.

If you focus on the characters, write about how the poets have created these verbal portraits. 'Looking at Miss World', 'Overheard in County Sligo', 'Growing Up', 'Young Woman Reassesses' are some of the poems you could consider.

The theme of parents and children crops up quite frequently in this section. (See, for example, 'You're', 'Praise Song for My Mother', 'Growing Up', 'The Railings' and 'Just Passing'.) If you take this theme, ask yourself what aspect each poem examines in the complicated and changing relationship between parents and children.

4 Symbols

Symbols are all around us: on maps, on street signs, in chemistry and algebra, on flags, in the words of our everyday speech and in poems. John Haines writes about 'the Green Man' (p. 55); Robert Herrick describes 'The Crosse-Tree' and sets out his poem in the shape of a cross (p. 84). Both are using symbols – words or phrases that describe an object or event that, in turn, refers to something beyond itself. In these two examples, the poets are referring to Spring and the Crucifixion.

Some symbols are common in everyday life, like 'the cross' or 'a red rose'. Poets use these conventional symbols, but many poets also create their own private and personal symbols. Roger McGough, for example, reworks the familiar symbol of 'the nails' from the Crucifixion (p. 160), while Seamus Heaney and Ted Hughes develop the personal symbolism of 'the peat bog' (p. 145) and the 'crow' (p. 141). There are other symbols, too: Gillian Clarke's 'box' (p. 115), and Sylvia Plath's 'mirror' (p. 104) and 'mushrooms' (p. 99).

Think about these symbols and what they represent. How have the poets used them to convey feelings and ideas?

Acknowledgements

Thanks are due to the authors (or their executors), their representatives and publishers mentioned in the following list for their kind permission to reproduce copyright material:

John Silkin: 'Caring for Animals' and 'Death of a Bird' from *Poems New and Selected* Chatto & Windus Ltd

Carl Sandburg: 'Wilderness' from *Cornhuskers*; 'Who do you think you are?' from *The People, Yes* Harcourt Brace Jovanovich Inc.

Douglas Livingstone: 'The King' from *Sjambok and Other Poems from Africa* © Oxford University Press 1964

Alan Brownjohn: 'Parrot' from *Brownjohn's Beasts*; 'The Rabbit' from *The Railings* the Digby Press and Macmillan, London and Basingstoke

Seamus Heaney: 'The Early Purges', 'Blackberry-Picking' and 'Digging' from *Death of a Naturalist*; 'Limbo' from *Wintering Out*; 'Bogland' from *Door into the Dark*, 'Personal Helicon' from *Death of a Naturalist*; 'From the Frontier of Writing' from *The Haw Lantern*; 'The Grauballe Man' and 'Punishment' from *North*; extract from 'Feeling into Words' from *Preoccupations: Selected Prose 1968–1978* Faber & Faber Ltd

May Swenson: 'The Secret in the Cat' from *Half Sun Half Sleep* by May Swenson, Copyright 1967 by May Swenson and Charles Cribner's Sons New York, reprinted by permission of the author

Malcolm Timperley for 'The Fan' and Graham Walley for 'Death of God' from *Ulula* The Manchester Grammar School

Theodore Roethke: 'Meadow Mouse' from *The Collected Poems* Faber & Faber Ltd. Copyright © 1963, 1961, 1960 by Beatrice Roethke, Administratrix of the Estate of Theodore Roethke from the book *Collected Poems of Theodore Roethke*. Reprinted by permission of Doubleday Company Inc.

John Haines: 'If the Owl Calls Again' and 'And When the Green Man Comes' from *Winter News* copyright © 1961, 1962 (by John Haines) Wesleyan University Press

Michael Benedikt: 'Thoughts' from *The Body* copyright © 1968 by Michael Benedikt, Wesleyan University Press

George Macbeth: 'Owl' by permission of the author

Walter de la Mare: 'Winter' and 'A Robin' by permission of The Literary Trustees of Walter de la Mare and The Society of Authors as their representative

Stevie Smith: 'Best Beast at the Fatstock Show' from *Frog Prince and Other Poems* Longman

Sylvia Plath: 'Mirror' from *Crossing the Water*; 'Mushrooms', 'A Winter Ship' and 'Metaphors' from *The Colossus*; 'Balloons', 'The Arrival of the Bee Box', 'Morning Song' and 'You're' from *Ariel* by courtesy of Miss Olwyn Hughes

Denise Levertov: 'To the Snake' from *Eyes at the Back of Our Heads*. Copyright © 1958 by Denise Levertov Goodman. Reprinted by permission of New Directions Publishing Corporation, New York and Laurence Pollinger Ltd and 'The Disclosure' from *O Taste and See*. Copyright © 1964 by Denise Levertov Goodman. Reprinted by permission of New Directions Publishing Corporation, New York

Emily Dickinson: 'Snake' reprinted by permission of the publishers and the Trustees of Amherst College from Thomas H Johnson, Editor *The Poems of Emily Dickinson*, Cambridge Mass: The Belknap Press of Harvard University Press, Copyright, 1951, 1955, by the President and Fellows of Harvard College

James Kirkup: 'Baby's Drinking Song' from *White Shadows Black Shadows* J M Dent & Sons Ltd

Tony Connor: 'A Child Half-Asleep' from *Kon In Springtime* © Oxford University Press 1968

R S Thomas 'Children's Song' from *Song at the Year's Turning* Granada Publishing Ltd

Robert Graves: 'Warning to Children' from *Collected Poems 1965* A P Watt & Son, by permission of Robert Graves

Stephen Spender: 'To My Daughter' from *Collected Poems 1928–1953*; 'Fifteen Line Sonnet in Four Parts' from *The Generous Days* Faber & Faber Ltd

Elaine Feinstein: 'At Seven a Son'; David Harsent: 'Rag Doll to the Heedless Child'; Jeremy Hooker: 'Winter Moon' from *Poetry Introduction 1* Faber & Faber Ltd (by permission of the authors)

Brian Jones: 'Thaw', 'How to Catch Tiddlers' and 'Visiting Miss Emily' from *Poems and a Family Album* London Magazine Editions

Liz Lochhead: 'Storyteller' from *Dreaming Frankenstein* Polygon

John Haines: 'The Cauliflower', 'In Nature' and 'Dreams of a Cardboard Lover' from *The Stone Harp* Andre Deutsch Ltd

William Meredith: 'Fledglings' from *Earth Walk: New and Selected Poems* Alfred A Knopff Inc.

Langston Hughes: 'The Ballad of the Landlord' from *Montage of a Dream Deferred* Harold Ober Associates; 'Dream Variation' from *Selected Poems* Alfred A Knopff Inc.

Douglas Dunn: 'Love Poem', 'On Roofs of Terry Street' and 'From the Night Window' from *Terry Street* Faber & Faber Ltd

Carol Ann Duffy: 'Valentine' from *Mean Time* Anvil Press Poetry Ltd 1993

Tony Harrison: 'Long Distance 2' from *Selected Poems* Penguin Books Ltd

G M Hopkins: 'Clouds' from *Diaries and Journals by G M Hopkins* Oxford University Press

Norman MacCaig: 'Summer Waterfall, Glendale' from *Measures*; 'Hotel Room, 12th Floor' from *Rings on a Tree*; 'Moorings' from *A Round of Applause* Chatto & Windus Ltd

George MacKay Brown: 'Weather Bestiary' from *The Year of the Whale* Chatto & Windus Ltd

Anthony Thwaite: 'A Haiku Yearbook' from *Inscriptions* Oxford University Press

Wes Magee: 'Sunday Morning' from *Poetry Introduction 2* Faber & Faber Ltd, by permission of the author

Philip Larkin: 'To the Sea' from *High Windows* Faber & Faber Ltd

Richard Ryan: 'A Heap of Stones' from *Poetry Introduction 2* Faber & Faber Ltd, first published by Dolmen Press, Dublin, reprinted by permission of the author

Roger McGough: 'Watchwords' and 'The Hippopotamusman' from *Watchwords* by Roger McGough, Jonathan Cape Ltd; 'Waving at Trains' from *Waving at Trains*, 'The Railings' from *After the Merrymaking* and 'Three Rusty Nails' from *In the Classroom* Jonathan Cape; 'Rabbit in Mixer Survives' *Daily Telegraph*; 'Just Passing' and 'Who are these men? from *Defying Gravity* Penguin Books Ltd. Reprinted by permission of Peters Fraser & Dunlop Group Ltd

Kenneth Rexroth: 'I return to the Place Where I was Born' by T'ao Yuan Ming from *Love and the Turning*